Maritime Security in East and West Africa

Dirk Siebels

Maritime Security in East and West Africa

A Tale of Two Regions

palgrave
macmillan

Dirk Siebels
Risk Intelligence A/S
Hellerup, Denmark

ISBN 978-3-030-22687-9 ISBN 978-3-030-22688-6 (eBook)
https://doi.org/10.1007/978-3-030-22688-6

This Palgrave Pivot imprint is published by the registered company Springer Nature Switzerland AG
The registered company address is: Gewerbestrasse 11, 6330 Cham, Switzerland

Acknowledgements

There is scant space to pay tribute to all those people who have provided ideas and material during years of research that have finally led to this book. I have not even tried to compile a complete list and would rather like to concentrate on some of the most pleasant experiences.

My first longer research trip to West Africa took me to the Kofi Annan International Peace Training Centre in Accra, Ghana, where any amount of time is well spent. All staff members and course participants are not just incredibly friendly, but also extremely knowledgeable about a broad variety of issues. Moreover, I was fortunate enough to meet never-tiring scholars like Albert Samah from Cameroon or Kamal-Deen Ali and Philip Attuquayefio from Ghana who get through monumental workloads on any given day, despite all the small and large problems that are far too common at most institution in sub-Saharan Africa.

Another organisation that deserves praise is the Maritime Security Centre of Excellence, hosted by the Turkish Navy and now based in Istanbul. I had the privilege to lecture there several times already and am very much looking forward to many more interesting seminars.

Compliments should also go to the brilliant staff at Risk Intelligence. Turning Ph.D.-level research into practical outputs is not something that should be taken for granted and I highly appreciate the opportunity to work for and with a bunch of people with an unbelievable amount of specialist knowledge on a daily basis.

Finally, the two most important cheers. One is to all the people throughout sub-Saharan Africa (in 'small countries with big stamps', as one of my friends once put it) who have shared their insights and—more often than not—something of their lives with me over the years. Much of the information I got over spicy food and local beers is never written down and can only be retrieved through the type of research that doesn't always look like actual work. If nothing else, I have learned one thing from these conversations: Africa is not a poor continent. It is blessed with vast natural and human resources, yet it is unfortunate that these riches have rarely been put to good use.

The second one goes to my family and especially my wife Katrin. She rarely buys the right type of chocolate, but never complains about obscure working hours and always tolerates my absences and distractedness, which I take for granted far too often. The boys and I are very lucky.

Contents

1 Introduction 1

2 Definitions and Available Literature 9

3 Lubricants for Development 31

4 A Victimless Crime 57

5 Growing Together 73

6 Contrasting Regions 101

7 Conclusion 129

Index 139

List of Figures

Fig. 2.1	Negative definition of maritime security	21
Fig. 2.2	Positive definition of maritime security	21
Fig. 3.1	World seaborne trade by volume 2006–2017, percentage share of Africa	41
Fig. 3.2	Hijackings off product tankers in 2011 off Cotonou and Lagos	44
Fig. 5.1	Maritime security incidents in West Africa (Senegal to Angola) recorded by different organisations, 2007–2018	78

List of Tables

Table 3.1 Oil rents (percentage of GDP) 36
Table 3.2 Public finances (percentage of GDP) for 2014 37
Table 3.3 Customs duties in tax revenue for selected countries in % 42
Table 5.1 Naval personnel in relation to armed forces personnel 76

CHAPTER 1

Introduction

Abstract This chapter introduces the main focus of the book: maritime security in East and West Africa. It points out that maritime issues in general have been largely ignored in both regions during the past decades. Complex relationships between different actors at sea are described very broadly and some examples—explored in detail throughout the following chapters—show that maritime developments often have direct implications on land. Furthermore, most challenges in the maritime environment are transnational by nature, such as oil and gas fields straddling maritime boundaries, migratory fish stocks that are exploited in different jurisdictions or attacks against merchant ships which may impact ports across an entire region. In the final section, the chapter underlines the importance of discussions about maritime security in relation to economic topics. Governments throughout sub-Saharan Africa stand to benefit from the blue economy's vast potential that would be a vital contribution to economic growth and development throughout sub-Saharan Africa. This potential has long been neglected and started to receive more attention only in recent years.

Keywords Maritime security · Sub-Saharan Africa · Blue economy

This book analyses the current state of maritime security in East and West Africa. Governments in both regions have more or less ignored the maritime environment for decades.[1] In recent years, however, three

D. Siebels, *Maritime Security in East and West Africa*,
https://doi.org/10.1007/978-3-030-22688-6_1

distinct developments have led to an increased interest in maritime issues: piracy off the Somali coastline, the growing importance of offshore oil and gas production, and an increasing interest in the sustainable exploitation of fish stocks along the coastline. These aspects were the main drivers behind the African Union's first-ever maritime summit which was held in the Togolese capital Lomé in October 2016.[2]

Despite an increasing amount of research about topics related to the maritime environment in general and maritime security in particular, academics and practitioners alike tend to concentrate on some selected subjects. In many cases, there may be good reasons for such a narrow focus. Unfortunately, more comprehensive observations of links between different actors and developments in the maritime environment as well as connections with land-based issues are still extremely rare.

The 'bigger picture' is important for decisions in a broad range of areas. Increasing offshore oil production, for example, can generate revenues for exporting countries,[3] yet challenges with financial transparency have to be addressed at the same time.[4] Some of the money can then be used to improve naval capabilities and to provide security around oil fields while additional patrol boats may also be used to identify and detain illegal fishing vessels. Such efforts would directly benefit small-scale fishermen along the coastline who are suffering from the impact of foreign fishing fleets.[5] At the same time, offshore installations can affect traditional fishing grounds. Local fishermen, afraid to lose their livelihoods, may then employ illegal methods themselves or supplement their income through smuggling and other illegal activities at sea.[6]

Even such a short description illustrates the complex interplay of various actors at sea. Decisions in one area often lead to unexpected developments in another. The same area of the sea can be used for different purposes, ranging from fishing and coastal tourism to merchant shipping and offshore oil production. Some of these purposes, such as small-scale fishing and coastal tourism, may complement each other, and others are directly linked with each other. Other activities, however, are mutually exclusive, for example fishing and offshore oil production.[7] Such issues may not be unique to the maritime environment, yet it certainly offers a worthwhile area for academic research.

On the national level, links between government agencies, local communities and the private sector—comprising local and international companies—have to be analysed. Local fishermen often know more about their immediate environment than naval or coastguard officers, even though their knowledge is rarely mentioned in discussions about maritime security.[8] Partnerships between the private and the public sector are necessary to fund large-scale infrastructure projects such as ports or offshore energy production, yet companies have to rely on the government to provide security.[9] Many other examples can be identified, some of which are explored in detail throughout this book.

Moreover, developments at sea not only have direct implications on land in specific countries, but also across a wider area, creating the need for cooperation on topics ranging from environmental regulations to joint naval patrols. Oil and gas fields might straddle maritime boundaries, for example between Nigeria and São Tomé and Príncipe[10] or between Senegal and Mauritania.[11] Migratory fish stocks are vulnerable to exploitation in one jurisdiction, impacting coastal communities in neighbouring countries.[12] Significant numbers of attacks against merchant ships can have a knock-on effect on ports throughout a region such as West Africa, making maritime trade more expensive.[13]

At the same time, maritime security—just as security in general—is a public good, leading to very basic questions. Who pays for maritime security and who benefits most from improvements? Compared with security on land, governments may feel less compelled to invest because a lack of maritime security does not have a direct impact on domestic populations. Furthermore, the problem of free-riding is not a new phenomenon, highlighted by a report on Chinese piracy, published in February 1867 in *The London and China Telegraph*:

> Besides we are not the only Power with large interests at stake. French, Americans, and Germans carry on an extensive trade [...] Why should we then incur singly the expense of suppressing piracy if each provided a couple of gunboats the force would suffice for the safety of foreign shipping which is all that devolves upon [...] why should the English tax payer alone bear the expense?[14]

Maritime developments in general and maritime security in particular have not been the topic of much academic research in the past, especially in sub-Saharan Africa. There is a sizeable gap in the academic literature; attention of scholars and practitioners has only increased in the past decade. Most of that attention can be attributed to piracy and armed robbery at sea off Somalia and in the Gulf of Guinea. Such incidents, however, should only be a small part of an overarching discussion about maritime security. Nevertheless, both regions offer interesting case studies. Efforts to improve maritime security differ, yet there are also similarities and lessons that have been learned and can now be applied in other parts of the world.

1.1 Structure of the Book

Throughout the next five chapters, this book provides a comprehensive look at different aspects which are closely related to maritime security in East and West Africa. Chapter 2 sets the scene and explains that there is currently no generally accepted definition of maritime security. It is often seen as part of traditional discussions about naval power, yet such discussions are completely irrelevant for most countries around the world, including coastal states in sub-Saharan Africa.

The following chapters then highlight why maritime security should be analysed in an economic rather than a security context. First and foremost, a secure environment at sea is a key aspect of the 'blue economy'. The economic potential of any country's maritime domain[15] can only be fully exploited when laws and regulations are in place and enforced by navies, coastguards or other agencies with a maritime remit.

Notable examples for the blue economy's potential to stimulate growth and economic development throughout Africa include offshore oil and gas production, maritime trade and fishing. These aspects are analysed for East and West Africa in Chapters 3 and 4, highlighting that improved security at sea can have direct benefits for government budgets, providing policymakers with additional resources to spend in areas such as education, health care or infrastructure.

In Chapter 5, efforts to improve regional cooperation related to maritime security are scrutinised. Differences between East Africa—where international involvement led to a narrow focus on counter-piracy operations—and West Africa—where governments have addressed a broad set of maritime security issues—are the focus of the analysis. The chapter also contains a discussion of the broader context for regional approaches. Governments often have different interests and administrative structures need to be aligned to create a secure maritime environment. Some relevant structures within regional economic communities already exist. It is therefore not necessary to duplicate frameworks or even create completely new organisations which are solely concerned with maritime issues.

Finally, Chapter 6 shows different options to improve maritime security on the national and regional level. The chapter includes a comprehensive list of recommendations for governments in East and West Africa as well as for international partners, non-governmental organisations and other actors with an interest in the maritime environment. Moreover, it highlights that maritime security in sub-Saharan Africa may be different than in other parts of the world, creating potential for unique partnerships between governments, domestic security agencies and the private sector.

1.2 Challenges and Opportunities

On a personal level, the author's interest in different aspects of maritime security was sparked by his experience as a naval officer. In many conversations with former and serving naval officers, the impression that few of them know much about the background of most vessels at sea was confirmed time and again. Interactions between naval personnel and crews on merchant vessels are rare. The same is true for fishing experts. Marine biologists are rarely invited to talk about implications of illegal fishing at conferences about maritime security or at courses for naval officers. Even basic fishing patterns, which can have a direct impact on other ships, are often a mystery to officers on naval or merchant vessels.

While there are exceptions to the rule, the situation has not changed significantly in recent years. Fishermen are widely regarded as a nuisance by naval personnel, rarely as a source of local knowledge. Boarding teams sent from navy ships to merchant vessels are often at a loss as military personnel are unable to read bills of lading, unfamiliar with the general construction and sometimes even confused by the small crew. Off the Somali coast, Nato navies used to offer protected convoys for merchant vessels, only to realise that operators would rather run the risk of a pirate attack than losing money by having their ships spend more time at sea.[16]

By and large, security issues on land receive much more attention than those at sea, especially in sub-Saharan Africa. Considering the ocean's economic potential, however, the discussion should shift at least to an extent. Governments throughout Africa—as well as in other regions around the world—can benefit from blue economy's potential. From trade to tourism, from fishing to energy production, the sea offers vast opportunities. These have long been ignored, leading to a lack of security at sea. It is therefore important to analyse why the oceans have been neglected for so long and to draw lessons for the future.

Notes

1. See, for example, Dunne, John Paul. "Order at sea and landlocked countries in Africa: Economic benefits." 115–118, in: Mandrup, Thomas and Very, Francois (eds.) *Towards good order at sea: African experiences*. Stellenbosch: Sun Media, 2015. 115–126; Hassan, Adam Abdou. 2018. The blue economy has become an indisputable reality for African countries. *ID4D*. Available at: https://ideas4development.org/en/blue-economy-reality-africa/.
2. Ndubisi, Adaobi. 2016. Togo to hold first maritime security summit in Africa. *The Cable*. Available at: https://www.thecable.ng/togo-hold-first-maritime-security-summit-africa.
3. Alike, Ejiofor. 2016. Nigeria: Kachikwu's U.S.$80 billion Chinese investment as a game changer. *All Africa*. Available at: https://allafrica.com/stories/201607050734.html; Ovadia, Jesse Salah. *The petro-developmental state in Africa: Making oil work in Angola, Nigeria and the Gulf of Guinea*. London: Hurst, 2016.
4. Sharife, Khadija. 2016. Exclusive: How Nigeria's lucrative deepwater oil profits disappear. *Business Live*. Available at: https://www.businesslive.co.za/fm/fm-fox/2016-04-28-exclusive-how-nigerias-lucrative-deepwater-oil-profits-disappear/.
5. Daniels, Gutiérrez, Fanjul, et al. *Western Africa's missing fish*. London: Overseas Development Institute, 2016. 10–15.
6. Interpol. *Study on fisheries crime in the West African coastal region*. Lyon: Environmental Security Sub-Directorate, Project Scale, 2014. 25–30.
7. Douvere, Fanny. 2008. "The importance of marine spatial planning in advancing ecosystem-based sea use management." *Marine Policy*, Vol. 32. 763–766.
8. Personal interview with Ghana Navy staff officer, May 2015.
9. World Bank. *Beyond the bottlenecks: Ports in Africa*. Africa Infrastructure Country Diagnostic—Background Paper 8. Washington: The World Bank, 2009. 39–41.
10. dos Santos, Gustavo Placido. 2015. Nigeria and Sao Tome and Principe: A relationship centered on oil and geostrategy—Analysis. *Eurasia Review*. Available at: https://www.eurasiareview.com/12092015-nigeria-and-sao-tome-and-principe-a-relationship-centered-on-oil-and-geostrategy-analysis/.
11. Diagana, Kissima. 2018. Senegal, Mauritania agree to cooperate on giant offshore gas field. *Reuters*. Available at: https://www.reuters.com/article/senegal-mauritania-gas/senegal-mauritania-agree-to-cooperate-on-giant-offshore-gas-field-idUSL8N1PZ6OY.

12. Bailey, Ishimura, Paisley, and Sumaila. 2013. "Moving beyond catch allocation approaches for internationally shared fish stocks." *Marine Policy*, Vol. 40. 124–125.
13. Burlando, Cristea, and Lee. 2015. "The trade consequences of maritime insecurity: Evidence from Somali piracy." *Review of International Economics*, Vol. 23:3. 525–526.
14. Quoted in: Besley, Fetzer, and Mueller. 2012. "One kind of lawlessness: Estimating the welfare cost of Somali piracy." Barcelona GSE Working Paper Series: Working Paper No. 626. 4.
15. Despite a widely used US definition, the term 'maritime domain' originally refers to the maritime zones that belong to a specific country, i.e. territorial waters, contiguous zone and exclusive economic zone. Areas beyond national jurisdiction are part of the maritime environment, but not part of any country's maritime domain.
16. Personal interview with former staff officer serving in EUNAVFOR, November 2014.

CHAPTER 2

Definitions and Available Literature

Abstract This chapter provides definitions for the geographical regions covered in this book and briefly discusses academic approaches to explain security integration within specific regions. It also introduces the concept of regional security complexes in relation to the analysis of security integration in East and West Africa. The concept is a helpful tool to analyse maritime security integration which has taken place in both regions over the past decade, even though it is still a much lower priority for most governments than land-based security threats. Furthermore, this chapter juxtaposes two possible definitions of maritime security. While a negative definition is merely based on the absence of threats, the positive definition—which is used here—regards maritime security as a desirable end state which creates various opportunities, notably for economic development. Exact topics for such a 'good order at sea' then have to be defined by governments, for example, through codes of conduct which have been adopted in East and West Africa.

Keywords East Africa · West Africa · Good order at sea · Ocean governance

Exact definitions for the topics covered in this book are hard to find. Nevertheless, geographic regions such as 'East' and 'West' Africa have to be defined to allow for meaningful research. The definitions used here are outlined in the first part of this chapter, followed by a summary of

D. Siebels, *Maritime Security in East and West Africa*,
https://doi.org/10.1007/978-3-030-22688-6_2

theories related to regional integration in general and security integration in particular.

Furthermore, the term 'maritime security' means different things to different people. No standard definition is available in the literature, a short definition of the term as it is used in this book is therefore provided below.

2.1 Regional Definitions

Definition of West Africa

For any geographic region without distinct natural boundaries, it is complicated to find a clear definition. The United Nations Statistics Division includes 16 African countries and the British Overseas Territory Saint Helena in its definition of 'West Africa'.[1] The list comprises all coastal states from Mauritania to Nigeria as well as the island nation of Cape Verde and three landlocked states (Burkina Faso, Mali, Niger).

McCaskie and Fage offer a slightly different definition in the *Encyclopædia Britannica*, leaving out Saint Helena but adding Chad among landlocked states as well as Cameroon and Equatorial Guinea as coastal states for Western Africa. They also stress that 'West Africa is primarily a political and economic designation and comprises all the areas considered here except Cameroon, Chad, Equatorial Guinea, and the Saharan parts of Mali, Mauritania, and Niger'.[2]

Judging from the member states of the Economic Community of West African States (ECOWAS), that statement is only partly correct. While Cameroon, Chad, Equatorial Guinea and Mauritania are not part of the organisation, Mali and Niger belong to the regional economic community. The latter two countries even use the same currency as six other ECOWAS members. The ECOWAS website points out that '[c]olonial boundaries are still reflected in modern boundaries between contemporary West African states, cutting across ethnic and cultural lines, often dividing single ethnic groups between two or more states',[3] further complicating a definition.

Creating a distinct definition of West Africa for the purposes of this book therefore has to be based on political documents rather than geography. The *Yaoundé Code of Conduct*, adopted in June 2013, is a vital document in this regard because it provides a definition of West Africa in a maritime context.[4] The abbreviated official title (*Code of Conduct concerning the repression of piracy, armed robbery against ships, and illicit maritime activity in West and Central Africa*) is based on the signing ceremony during a summit in Cameroon's capital Yaoundé.

As stated in the title, the code is concerned with maritime security in West and Central Africa, yet Central Africa is not easily defined either. The UN Statistics Division, for example, provides a definition for 'Middle Africa' that contains nine countries: all coastal states from Cameroon to Angola, the island nation of São Tomé and Príncipe, and two landlocked states (Central African Republic, Chad). All these countries are members of the regional economic community for Central Africa (Economic Community of Central African States [ECCAS]) but two other landlocked nations, Rwanda and Burundi, are also ECCAS members.[5]

For the purposes of this book, the *Yaoundé Code of Conduct* is the guideline for a geographic definition of West Africa. Moreover, the entire region is referred to as 'West Africa' rather than the more cumbersome 'West and Central Africa'.

The *Yaoundé Code of Conduct* was adopted by members of three regional organisations: ECOWAS, ECCAS and the Gulf of Guinea Commission (GGC). Since all GGC members[6] are either part of ECOWAS or of ECCAS, the membership of the latter two organisations can be used as a regional definition for West Africa. For the purposes of this book, West Africa therefore comprises all coastal states and island nations between Senegal in the north and Angola in the south.

Definition of East Africa

Providing a geographical definition of East Africa that is relevant in the context of this book is similarly complicated. In its definition for Eastern Africa, the United Nations Statistics Division includes 20 territories: all coastal states between Eritrea and Mozambique, several landlocked states (Burundi, Ethiopia, Malawi, Rwanda, South Sudan, Uganda, Zambia, Zimbabwe), the islands of Réunion and Mayotte (French *départements*), and four island nations in the Indian Ocean (Comoros, Madagascar, Mauritius and the Seychelles).[7] In contrast, the *Encyclopædia Britannica* defines the region as 'part of sub-Saharan Africa comprising two traditionally recognized regions: East Africa, made up of Kenya, Tanzania, and Uganda; and the Horn of Africa, made up of Somalia, Djibouti, Eritrea, and Ethiopia'.[8]

Membership of regional economic communities does not offer much help regarding a definition for the region. These organisations include the Intergovernmental Authority on Development (IGAD), the East African Community (EAC) and the Southern African Development Community (SADC). Several countries are members of different organisations, for example, Kenya, South Sudan and Uganda (IGAD and EAC) or Tanzania (EAC and SADC).[9]

Some regional economic communities have already begun to integrate military capabilities. Cooperation is largely related to the African Standby Force, a peacekeeping force to be used by the African Union in response to armed conflicts on the continent.[10] While the concept itself is not vital for this book, it is useful to note that both ECOWAS and ECCAS have pledged to participate and to develop necessary capabilities by expanding regional cooperation. In East Africa, regional arrangements are different due to the complicated organisational landscape.[11] The same can be said for arrangements related to maritime security.

Another possible definition can be drawn from the *Djibouti Code of Conduct*, a similar document to the code for West Africa mentioned above.[12] Contents will be analysed throughout this book but compared with West Africa, the code is not particularly helpful regarding a definition of the region, underlined by the full title of the document: *Code of Conduct concerning the repression of piracy and armed robbery against ships in the Western Indian Ocean and the Gulf of Aden*. Overall, 21 countries were eligible to sign the document and only France (eligible because of the overseas territories of Réunion and Mayotte) decided not to get directly involved.

Signatories of the Djibouti Code of Conduct include all coastal states from Egypt to South Africa as well as landlocked Ethiopia, island nations in the Indian Ocean (Comoros, Madagascar, Maldives, Mauritius, Seychelles), and countries in the Middle East (Jordan, Oman, Saudi Arabia, United Arab Emirates, Yemen). Opening up the code to such a broad range of participants may have made sense at the time because the original document was solely concerned with the fight against piracy in the Indian Ocean. For the purposes of this book, however, the definition of East Africa as a region has to be more condensed to allow for meaningful comparisons with West Africa. The definition is still different from similar definitions, for example, the regional security complex around the Horn of Africa as defined by Buzan and Wæver.[13]

This book will focus on efforts in the African signatories of the Djibouti Code of Conduct. Two countries on the continent are not included in the analysis, namely Egypt and South Africa. While a discussion about maritime security in these countries is certainly important, their situation is entirely different from the region covered here. Both countries have relatively well-developed naval capabilities and can provide assistance to regional partners. At the same time, they are less affected by problems other countries along the East African coastline are facing, explained in detail throughout the following chapters.

2.2 Security Integration and Regional Security Complexes

Many theories in the academic field of international relations (IR)—including some offering conflicting viewpoints—can be used to analyse regional integration in general and security integration in particular. These may in turn be helpful to evaluate developments in the maritime security environment in East and West Africa. Theories ranging from realism and neofunctionalism to liberal institutionalism and social constructivism offer explanations for certain aspects, yet there is no one-size-fits-all approach when it comes to maritime security in both regions. Moreover, virtually all IR theories contain a largely Western perspective, 'based on a Euro-centric understanding of the past, the present and future'.[14]

In general, IR theories are based on a specific timeframe of European history, the so-called Westphalian era. As such, there is a preconceived idea of the world divided into sovereign states. In many regions around the globe, however, borders were imposed by colonial masters, disrupting political and societal structures. Borders in sub-Saharan Africa have rarely been shifted or redrawn after independence but are often less entrenched than in Europe.[15] Interactions on the political, economic and societal level therefore look different from similar interactions in the Western world,[16] posing a challenge to an analysis through a largely Western perspective. Acharya and Buzan underline the problem, stating that 'history matters (…) (and) even a short reflection on Western IRT [international relations theory] quickly exposes that much of it is conspicuously drawn from the model provided by modern European history'.[17]

The academic literature covering different aspects of security in Africa has grown over the past decade.[18] Nevertheless, the amount of theory-building articles and books is still negligible compared to academic works about security cooperation within Asia or, most notably, Europe. A similar picture emerges when the net is cast a little wider as James Meek has noted in his endorsement for Michael Peel's book *A swamp full of dollars*: 'Russia is an enigmatic petrochemical power with a population of 140 million; Nigeria is an enigmatic petrochemical power with a population of 140 million. Last year [2008] the British Library added almost 500 new Russia-related titles to its collection, and fewer than three dozen about Nigeria'.[19]

Analysing Regional Integration

Based on the limitations of IR theory, this segment provides a brief look at different strands and their limits when applied to regional integration in the African context. Some of the shortcomings are pointed out to sketch an outline for future discussions and research.

Realism is an important IR framework for regional security integration. In general, realist thinkers agree that the nation state is the most important actor on the international stage and that any state strives to protect its national interests. Waltz has defined power in a realist sense as something that 'provides the means of maintaining one's autonomy in the face of force that others wield'.[20] Mearsheimer has added that countries 'strive to gain power over their rivals',[21] by both economic and military means.

Modern realist thinkers base their assumptions on a concept largely rooted in the Cold War era, although states as anarchic actors which may form alliances long pre-date that. Following realist lines of thinking, the desire to control or fear of domination induces nations to act. While it may be premature to argue that the international system after the Cold War cannot be analysed based on realist assumptions,[22] these have never been high on the agenda of governments in sub-Saharan Africa. Henderson has tried to define an 'African Realism' yet his book is mainly concerned with international conflicts on the continent in the post-colonial era, largely leaving out domestic struggles and civil wars.[23] However, the number of interstate conflicts in sub-Saharan Africa has been dwarfed by the number of intra-state conflicts. Regime security has subsequently been a much more pressing concern than domination of other countries.[24]

Liberalism challenges the idea of a nation state with a certain set of national interests. While states are seen as important actors on the international stage, they are not regarded as unitary entities but rather as interdependent actors with a need to coordinate actions through common rules and institutions. Bull has defined the international order as a pattern of activity sustaining the goals of all nation states.[25] That includes maintaining the independence of states, preserving the system and limiting violent interactions. It is a fundamentally optimistic theory and regards regional or international cooperation as potentially unlimited.

Again, this concept cannot be applied easily to regional security integration in Africa. Even if supported by political will for more integration, which has often been lacking, limited capacities and resources constrain states trying to achieve deeper integration.[26] Moreover, different views on the need for integration can be traced back several decades and conflicts continue to linger.

Growing interdependence between nation states and the increasing importance of non-state actors has contributed to the development of institutionalism as another theoretical framework. It combines positive assumptions about cooperation between international actors with an emphasised role of formal institutions. They provide a framework for negotiations and shared information, yet are not merely passive tools. Institutions matter because they can shape opinions, actions and political developments over time.

Most of the literature on institutionalism uses developments within the European Union as the primary example for an institution that is constantly shaping politics in its member states.[27] Regime theory provides a similar framework, although based on realism. Krasner has defined international cooperation, for example, in areas such as security or trade, as regimes with certain norms, rules and procedures.[28] These will then help to facilitate a convergence of states' expectations.

Some examples for integration through common rules and institutions can indeed be found in Africa. At the same time, the institutional capacity of regional and continental organisations is limited at best.[29] Regional economic communities such as ECOWAS in West Africa or the EAC may have a secretariat, but no pool of bureaucrats or subject-matter experts that is comparable to the European Union. Such organisations often rely on host nations and foreign donors instead, thus limiting their ability to shape political debates.

Functionalism offers a slightly different outlook on regional integration. This theory is first and foremost concerned with functional cooperation in non-controversial areas. Social, technical or humanitarian aspects could be discussed between national governments and cooperation may spill over into other political fields. Initially, functionalism was introduced after the First World War, neofunctionalism later refined some assumptions.[30] The theory is mostly applied to the development of the European Union but it has been used to explain the development of other international organisations, usually dominated by Western nations.

In the African context, similar limitations as for institutionalism apply. Limited bureaucratic capacities restrict spillover effects of cooperation between governments. Furthermore, political will to initiate such cooperation is often lacking because the primary focus of many governments in sub-Saharan Africa is internal. In a private conversation with the author, a West African diplomat provided a vivid comparison: 'In West Africa, we are neighbours and live behind a fence. We barely talk, but we go to the same mosque or church. In Europe, neighbours argue over tiny things, but they also celebrate and develop friendships'.[31]

Theories for African Integration?

This brief look at different approaches to analyse regional integration is not a complete list. Nevertheless, it underlines that there are many attempts to explain why and how nation states may decide to work together, even in sensitive areas such as security politics. Realist theories aside, all concepts replace simple power politics with international or supranational frameworks. They question the overwhelming importance of 'hard power', emphasised by realists as an answer to centuries of state-centred politics by European powers.

At the same time, the overview indicates fundamental shortcomings when regional integration in Africa is explained through a lens that was, by and large, intended for the Western world. Limited institutional capacities, close ties to former colonial powers rather than neighbouring countries and a pronounced focus on internal affairs are merely three distinguishing factors between states in Europe and sub-Saharan Africa. It may be possible to explain some political developments in East and West Africa with traditional IR frameworks. Every analysis, however, will be flawed unless it notes potential shortcomings of a theoretical approach in a setting for which it was not originally developed.

Predictions are equally complicated. Whereas the analysis of European integration may offer analytical background for future developments, regional integration in Africa requires a different approach. Søren

Dosenrode has even summarised that 'when looking at the African Union and its high aspirations of African unity there is no theoretical framework to guide the statesmen embarking on it'.[32]

Explaining Regional Security Integration

Which theoretical approaches can explain security integration on the regional level, particularly in East and West Africa? One of the key works in this area was written by Barry Buzan and Ole Wæver. *Regions and Powers: the Structure of International Security*, published in 2003, is part of the Copenhagen School approach to IR theory. It attempts to divide the world into regional security complexes. Both East and West Africa are relatively well-defined examples, yet the definitions of both regions are different to those used here because Buzan and Wæver have concentrated on land-based developments.[33]

Before discussing the application of regional security complex theory, the failure of other theoretical frameworks to explain security integration should be mentioned. Various theories of European integration, notably intergovernmentalism or neofunctionalism, have long upheld the basic assumption that defence and security are policy areas with a specific character compared to economic or environmental issues. National governments 'would not give up their autonomous decision-making power in these questions to common institutions or supranational authorities'[34] because defence and security are regarded as core areas of national sovereignty.

Cooperation on a selective range of defence issues aside, most academics and practitioners failed to foresee the current level of integration in foreign and security politics within the European Union. Overall, the EU's Common Security and Defence Policy has demonstrated that integration is indeed possible and may be linked with other foreign policy strands.[35] Over the last decade, academics therefore had to adjust their theories to show that these may be used to explain future developments in different areas of European integration, including security. However, attempts to develop Euro-centric theories to explain developments—or the lack thereof—in African security integration are virtually non-existent, creating an enormous gap in the academic literature.

One notable exception is the work of Buzan and Wæver. Their premise is that most security threats will occur in a specific region. Connections between states and other actors in the region rarely concern outside actors. Any regional security complex can then be regarded as a micro-system where different IR theories may be applied.

In the chapter about sub-Saharan Africa, Buzan and Wæver acknowledge that 'the main focus of security in Africa is domestic – or more accurately substate'.[36] Conflict formations and patterns of alignment can be found 'much more at the substate level than at the interstate one',[37] creating a unique situation. West Africa in particular has been 'characterized by relative international peace and by domestic war'[38] since the former colonies became independent.

The security landscape has developed since *Regions and Powers* was published. Most importantly, the African Union created a framework to promote peace and security on the continent, built upon the existing infrastructure of regional economic communities. Whether the description of East and West Africa as proto-complexes provided by Buzan and Wæver in 2003 is still valid is therefore open for debate.

More importantly, an essential aspect of this book has not been mentioned by Buzan and Wæver at all. Maritime security may bring together a different set of actors within a region or across the traditional borders of any security complex. Landlocked nations—such as Mali and Chad in West Africa or Ethiopia and Uganda in East Africa—may be important for a regional security complex, yet they can be almost disregarded for discussions about maritime security. At the same time, island nations such as Cape Verde and São Tomé and Príncipe in West Africa or the Seychelles and Mauritius in East Africa are almost insignificant for developments on land but can make vital contributions to maritime issues.

One of the few examples in which regional security complex theory has been applied in a maritime context is a book by Manoj Gupta, published in 2010. The author presents a comprehensive overview over different governance regimes in the Indian Ocean region and security regimes are mentioned in one chapter in an attempt to 'establish intra-ocean patterns of relationship in conceptualising the Indian Ocean as a region'.[39] Four distinct regional security complexes (Horn of Africa, Middle East, South Asia and East Asia) had been identified earlier by Buzan and Wæver, yet little interaction exists between those regions. The maritime focus Gupta employs does not change that, but a certain degree of interaction can be identified, largely based on common economic interests.

Compared with other models in IR theory, regional security complex theory offers an entirely different approach. It is first and foremost concerned with the definition of certain regions where various IR models may then be applied. It does not create a contest between competing attempts to explain security developments. Instead, it may be used to identify a region based on the interplay between different actors which can then be analysed by appropriate theoretical frameworks.

2.3 Defining Maritime Security

The term 'maritime security' has not been used in a systematic way in the academic literature. In short, it means different things to different people. Geoffrey Till has underlined that more than two decades ago by pointing out a 'particular need to be clear about what is necessary for future maritime security and prosperity' while acknowledging that it 'is a far from easy task since the phrase "maritime security" comprehends so much'.[40] In a more recent publication (*Seapower: A Guide for the Twenty-First Century*), Till has suggested a distinction between 'hard security'—which regards the ocean as a 'source of power and dominion'—and 'soft security' which is concerned with natural resources, maritime trade and transportation.[41]

Other authors have also pointed out that there is no general consensus about the definition of maritime security.[42] On the one hand, it could be identified as a dimension of security. On the other hand, various dimensions of security may apply in the maritime environment as they possess a maritime element.[43] It is therefore possible to analyse, for example, maritime economic security or maritime environmental security, yet 'there appears to be no commonly accepted definition of what constitutes maritime security'.[44] This idea is nevertheless consistent with the broader view of security that has been developed after the Cold War.

In the aftermath of the terrorist attacks in the United States in September 2001, maritime security became a vital aspect of national security, reflected in the introduction of the ISPS Code to protect ports and merchant ships from terrorist attacks.[45] However, there is a clear legal distinction between piracy and maritime terrorism, even though perpetrators may use similar means. In Article 101, the 1982 United Nations Convention on the Law of the Sea (UNCLOS) defines piracy as an act committed for 'private ends' on the high seas.[46] The concept of the high seas used in UNCLOS goes back to the work of Hugo Grotius, the first proponent of 'The Free Sea' (*Mare Liberum*) in the seventeenth century.[47] By extension, acts classified as armed robbery at sea are similar in nature but take place within territorial waters.

Maritime terrorism is committed by individuals trying to make ideological or political points rather than acting for private ends,[48] both in territorial waters and on the high seas. This legal lacuna was filled by the 1988 *Convention for the suppression of unlawful acts against the safety of maritime navigation* (generally abbreviated to *SUA Convention*). By and large, however, terrorist attacks against merchant vessels or port facilities have remained a virtual threat[49] while rising numbers of pirate attacks off Somalia underlined a different maritime security challenge from 2007 onwards.

The threat of Somali piracy for international shipping may have been exaggerated,[50] but it led to discussions about maritime aspects of security and challenges to 'good order at sea'. While this is often used as a catch-all phrase without a coherent definition,[51] it broadly describes the aspects discussed here: secure transport of goods by sea, protection of resources in and under the ocean, and multinational cooperation to avoid exploitation of the sea by criminal or terrorist groups. Tensions between states, for example, in the Arctic or the South China Sea, have also increased attention for maritime security as a challenge with various dimensions.[52]

Broadly speaking, the term maritime security can therefore be defined in two ways. The negative definition (see Fig. 2.1) refers to the absence of threats such as terrorism, piracy, smuggling, IUU fishing or conflicts over maritime boundaries. Discussions concerned with maritime security often include some or all of these threats,[53] yet this approach is insufficient. Neighbouring countries may prioritise different issues, complicating cooperation to tackle a lack of maritime security. Moreover, the mere absence of threats does not show how certain issues may be linked and should be addressed.

Defining maritime security in a positive way offers better opportunities for cooperation between national governments and other stakeholders in the maritime environment (see Fig. 2.2). This approach defines the ocean—or at least territorial waters and EEZ—as an area where the rule of law is imposed, ensuring that the sea does not become ungoverned space. Maritime security thus becomes a desirable end state which requires threats to be addressed by necessary and sustainable means.

This approach has been criticised for a lack of theoretical considerations as 'the discussion turns immediately to questions of how law

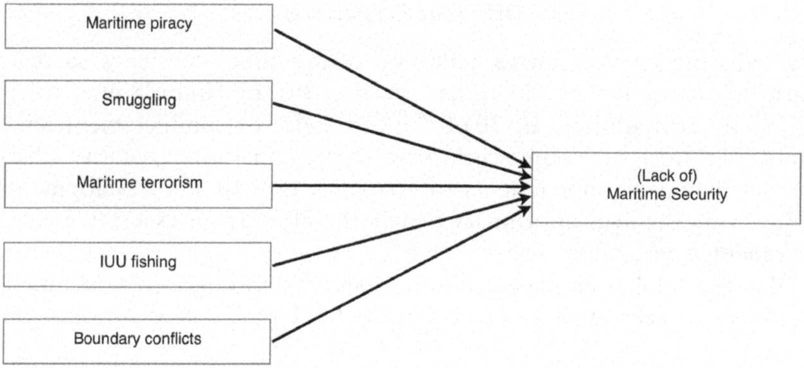

Fig. 2.1 Negative definition of maritime security (*Source* Author's diagram)

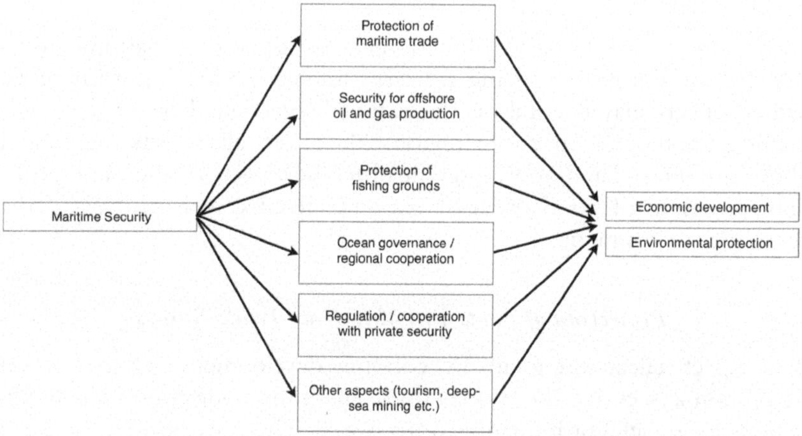

Fig. 2.2 Positive definition of maritime security (*Source* Author's diagram)

enforcement at sea can be improved'.[54] Theoretical discussions of 'good order at sea', however, are hardly necessary. These are addressed by international conventions and treaties, notably UNCLOS. On the African continent, the codes mentioned above also show how governments define maritime security on the regional level. Other regions may have different priorities, yet it is *their* order, defined in negotiations and in line with international law.

Different Perspectives

For this book, the positive definition of maritime security is particularly relevant, further underlined by the African Union's own maritime strategy, adopted in 2014.[55] Both codes of conduct mentioned above fit into this framework that regards maritime security challenges mainly as impediments to economic growth and development. Improving the lives of ordinary people therefore requires a stable environment at sea.

For this book, four main prisms are identified through which maritime security—as defined above—can be viewed in East and West Africa:

- protection of ports and maritime trade routes;
- security for offshore oil and gas production;
- protection of fishing grounds;
- ocean governance and regional cooperation.

This list is not exclusive, but it includes aspects of maritime security that are the most pressing concerns for many African governments. Other aspects may be vital on the national level, yet they are not overarching themes for an entire region. Moreover, all aspects mentioned above are interrelated and represent different aspects of the same problem: provision of good order at sea and effective management of the maritime environment.

Protection of Ports and Maritime Trade Routes

This aspect reflects the focus on economic development. While it is part of economic security, the protection of maritime trade routes has implications for societal or human security as well. These are beyond the focus of this book but certainly warrant further research.

Maritime piracy has been the focus of academic and public debates in recent years. Maritime security has often been reduced to the protection of merchant ships and the prosecution of pirates.[56] However, piracy has never been a strategic threat for the global economy[57] and even less so for coastal states in sub-Saharan Africa. Creating international task forces to conduct counter-piracy operations in the Indian Ocean was the equivalent of creating a police force that is solely responsible for bank robberies but does not investigate any other crimes.

For African nations, the real threat is closer to home. Merchant ships are often attacked at anchorages or even at berth, port security is limited and there are gaps between offshore and onshore security. Such an environment creates opportunities for criminals and corrupt officials, hampering economic development much more than perpetrators operating at sea.

Security for Offshore Oil and Gas Production

Offshore oil and gas production is another aspect of maritime security with an economic impact. Unlike the protection of maritime trade, however, it is strongly linked to national security. For many governments, revenues from the oil and gas industry are vital, underlined by military protection for company assets.[58] Maritime security may become even more important for the industry because an increasing share of oil and gas is likely to be produced offshore.[59]

Effective provision of security requires national and regional efforts. Offshore hydrocarbon deposits are often located close to maritime boundaries which still have to be defined in some cases. In many countries, the industry's strategic importance has created a demand for better protection of offshore assets, even though these are generally exploited by private companies.

Protection of Fishing Grounds

Throughout sub-Saharan Africa, fishing is vital for coastal communities. Fishermen's livelihoods, however, are threatened by illegal, unreported and unregulated (IUU) fishing that takes place in the EEZ or even in territorial waters. Foreign vessels are able to exploit fishing grounds because navies or coastguards lack capacities to enforce rules and regulations at sea.[60]

The protection of fish stocks is often regarded as an aspect of environmental security and has received much less attention than efforts to fight against maritime piracy. However, fish is also a natural resource that provides economic benefits.[61] Unlike offshore oil and gas, well-managed fish stocks replenish themselves. Moreover, artisanal fishing provides many employment opportunities, underlining the impact on national security because a lack of jobs in fishing communities may force some community members to engage in illicit activities.

Reliable information on IUU fishing is limited, making it complicated to consider actual impacts. New technology, however, helps researchers to gather data and draw conclusions about the amounts of fish caught without knowledge of government agencies and to increase transparency within the fishing industry.[62]

Ocean Governance and Regional Cooperation

With countries in both East and West Africa suffering from weak maritime governance, security in both regions is at least worrying for international actors.[63] It is therefore vital to explore relationships between governments, regional and international organisations, the private sector and other stakeholders. Security measures at sea may be necessary yet they are not sufficient. Lasting solutions have to be found on land before they can be translated into effective law enforcement at sea. Furthermore, regional cooperation is the key to solving problems rather than merely shifting them.

While UNCLOS and other global conventions provide some stability for ocean governance, there are no international solutions to ensure the enforcement of such documents. Standing naval forces under international command, for example, are very likely to remain fantasy for the foreseeable future. Regional solutions are therefore necessary to enforce existing rules and regulations. One major challenge for sub-Saharan Africa in particular is the fact that most governments lack expertise, assets and human resources to effectively deal with maritime issues—including maritime security—on the national level.

The African Union has taken first steps to improve ocean governance around the continent, underlined by its maritime strategy adopted in 2014. Some regional economic communities have also started to improve cooperation. Developments related to maritime security, particularly the two codes of conduct for East and West Africa, are examples for opportunities and challenges.

Synopsis

Different perspectives are an indicator for the manifold topics for discussions related to the positive definition of maritime security used in this book. Moreover, they can be attributed to different dimensions of security.

Military security is one dimension that is notably missing. Discussions about naval power are almost irrelevant in the African context. In most countries in sub-Saharan Africa, the navy is hardly able to operate throughout the EEZ, let alone conduct military operations against other countries. Using a classification system that includes ten ranks of capabilities between global-reaching power projection and a token presence on inland waterways,[64] naval forces in East and West Africa generally rank close to the bottom of the scale. In short, it is unlikely that they will affect the military security of neighbouring countries.

Maritime security as defined in this book therefore follows a non-traditional approach. The topic is analysed through several prisms with unique characteristics. At the same time, different perspectives are interrelated, underlining that maritime issues are generally linked on the national and the regional level.

From an international point of view, the perspective on maritime security in East and West Africa may be different. Counter-piracy operations in the Indian Ocean have been high-profile missions in recent years, other aspects of maritime security have been widely ignored. One of the questions addressed in this book therefore is whether international actors are only concerned with security threats that directly impact them.

2.4 Summary

Maritime security is a key aspect of the 'blue economy'. It should therefore be analysed in an economic rather than a purely military context, partly because economic growth increases government revenues which are needed to build and maintain naval capacities to ensure maritime security.

Furthermore, the discussion above underlines that this book is an essential contribution to ongoing academic and political discussions. Maritime security in East and West Africa as well as regional security integration in general have received little attention in the past. The range of challenges that governments in both regions are facing, however, merits a comprehensive analysis. This book aims to address at least some of the existing gaps in the available literature, providing an important contribution to ongoing and future debates.

Notes

1. United Nations Statistics Division. 2019. Methodology—Standard country or area codes for statistical use. Available at: https://unstats.un.org/unsd/methodology/m49/.
2. McCaskie, T. C. and Fage, John D. 2019. Western Africa. Encyclopaedia Britannica. Available at: https://www.britannica.com/place/western-Africa.
3. ECOWAS. 2019. Member states. Available at: http://www.ecowas.int/member-states/.
4. International Maritime Organizsation. 2019. Code of Conduct concerning the repression of piracy, armed robbery against ships, and illicit maritime activity in West and Central Africa, signed in Yaoundé on 25 June 2013. Available at: http://www.imo.org/en/OurWork/Security/WestAfrica/Documents/code_of_conduct%20signed%20from%20ECOWAS%20site.pdf.
5. United Nations Economic Commission for Africa. 2019. ECCAS— Economic Community of Central African States. Available at: https://www.uneca.org/oria/pages/eccas-economic-community-central-african-states.
6. Gulf of Guinea Commission. 2019. The Gulf of Guinea Commission. Available at: https://cggrps.com/en/the-gulf-of-guinea-commission/#.
7. United Nations Statistics Division. 2019. Methodology—Standard country or area codes for statistical use. Available at: https://unstats.un.org/unsd/methodology/m49/.
8. Low, A. Anthony and Marcus, Harold G. 2019. Eastern Africa. Encyclopaedia Britannica. Available at: https://www.britannica.com/place/eastern-Africa.
9. An overlap can also be found in West Africa where Angola and DR Congo are members of SADC and ECCAS.
10. Darkwa, Linda. 2017. "The African Standby Force: The African Union's tool for the maintenance of peace and security." *Contemporary Security Policy*, Vol. 38. 471–482.
11. Aboagye, Festus. 2012. "A stitch in time would have saved nine—Operationalising the African Standby Force." ISS Policy Brief No. 34.
12. International Maritime Organizsation. 2019. The Djibouti Code of Conduct. Available at: http://www.imo.org/en/OurWork/Security/PIU/Pages/Content-and-Evolution-of-the-Djibouti-Code-of-Conduct.aspx.
13. Buzan, Barry and Wæver, Ole. *Regions and powers: The structure of international security*. Cambridge: Cambridge University Press, 2003. 233–247.
14. Theory Talks. 2009. Barry Buzan on international society, securitization, and an English school map of the world. Available at: http://www.theory-talks.org/2009/12/theory-talk-35.html.

15. Nugent, Paul. *Africa since independence—A comparative history*, Basingstoke: Palgrave Macmillan, 2012. 448–506.
16. A concise discussion of governance standards in developing countries can be found in: Thomas, M. A. *Govern like us*. New York: Columbia University Press, 2015.
17. Acharya, Amitav and Buzan, Barry. 2007. "Why is there no non-Western international relations theory? An introduction." *International Relations of the Asia-Pacific*, Vol. 7:3. 289.
18. Noteworthy examples include: Williams, Paul D. *War and conflict in Africa*. Cambridge: Polity Press, 2011; Aning, Kwesi and Pokoo, John. 2014. "Understanding the nature and threats of drug trafficking to national and regional security in West Africa". *Stability: International Journal of Security & Development*, Vol. 3:1. 1–13; Coleman, Katharina P. and Tieku, Thomas K. (eds.). *African actors in international security: Shaping contemporary norms*. Boulder: Lynne Rienner, 2018; Karbo, Tony and Murithi, Tim (eds.). *The African Union—Autocracy, diplomacy and peacebuilding in Africa*. London: I.B. Tauris, 2018. Other authors have analysed the development of the African Peace and Security Architecture by the African Union since 2002, for example, Francis, David (ed.). *Peace & conflict in Africa*. London: Zed Books, 2008; Vines, Alex. 2013. "A decade of African peace and security architecture." *International Affairs*, Vol. 89:1. 89–109; Engel, Ulf and Gomes Porto, Joao. 2014. "Imagining, implementing, and integrating the African peace and security architecture: The African Union's challenges." *African Security*, Vol. 7:3. 135–146; and Appiah, Juliana Abena. 2018. "Africa peace and security architecture: Reflection on over a decade of promoting peace and security in Africa." *Africa Insight*, Vol. 47:4. 29–39.
19. Peel, Michael. *A swamp full of dollars*. London: I.B. Tauris, 2009. i.
20. Waltz, Kenneth. *Theory of international politics*. London: McGraw-Hill. 194.
21. Mearsheimer, John. "Anarchy and the struggle for power." 56, in: Art, R. J. and Jervis, R. (eds.) *International politics: Enduring concepts and contemporary issues—Eighth Edition*. London: Pearson Longman, 2001. 50–60.
22. Westad, Odd Arne. "Introduction: Reviewing the Cold War." 7–11, in: Westad, Odd Arne (ed.) *Reviewing the Cold War—Approaches, interpretations, theory*. London: Routledge, 2000. 1–26.
23. Henderson, Errol. *African realism? International relations theory and Africa's wars in the postcolonial era*. Lanham: Rowman & Littlefield, 2015.
24. Baumu, Evarist and Sturman, Kathryn. 2010. "Amendment to the African Union's right to intervene." *African Security Review*, Vol. 12:2. 39–42.

25. Bull, Hedley. *The anarchical society: A study of order in world politics.* New York: Columbia University Press, 1985. 8–19.
26. de Melo, Jaime and Tsikata, Yvonne. *Regional integration in Africa—Challenges and prospects.* Helsinki: WIDER, 2014. 7–11.
27. Rosamond, Ben. *Theories of European integration.* Basingstoke: Palgrave, 2000. 98–129.
28. Krasner, Stephen. *International regimes.* Ithaca: Cornell University Press, 1983. 141.
29. Nganje, Fritz. *Moving beyond Africa's crisis of institutions.* Johannesburg: SAIIA, 2015. 14–18.
30. Mitrany, David. *The functional theory of politics.* New York: St. Martin's Press, 1976; Rosamond, Ben. *Theories of European integration.* Basingstoke: Palgrave, 2000. 50–73.
31. Personal interview with West African government representative, November 2018.
32. Dosenrode, Søren. 2010. "Federalism theory and Neo-functionalism: Elements for an analytical framework". *Perspectives on Federalism,* Vol. 2:3. 3.
33. Buzan and Wæver. *Regions and powers.* 231.
34. Ojanen, Hanna. *Theories at a loss? EU-NATO fusion and the 'low-politicisation' of security and defence in European integration.* Helsinki: FIIA, 2002. 4.
35. Koutrakos, Panos. *The EU common security and defence policy.* Oxford: Oxford University Press, 2013. 210–247.
36. Buzan and Wæver. *Regions and powers.* 228.
37. Buzan and Wæver. *Regions and powers.* 299.
38. Kacowicz, Arie. *Zones of peace in the third world: South America and West Africa in comparative perspective.* New York: State University of New York Press, 1998. 125.
39. Gupta, Manoj. *Indian Ocean region: Maritime regimes for regional cooperation.* New York: Springer, 2010. 10.
40. Till, Geoffrey. "Developments in Maritime Security." 5, in: Cozens, Peter (ed.) *New Zealand's maritime environment and security.* Wellington: Centre for Strategic Studies, 1994. 5–27.
41. Till, Geoffrey. *Seapower: A guide for the twenty-first century.* London: Routledge, 2013. 310–311.
42. Examples include: Klein, Natalie. *Maritime security and the law of the sea.* Oxford: Oxford University Press, 2011. 2–11; Kraska, James, and Pedrozo, Raul. *International maritime security law.* Leiden: Martinus Nijhoff, 2013. 12–15.
43. Chalk, Peter. *The maritime dimension of international security: Terrorism, piracy and challenges for the United States.* Santa Monica: RAND Corporation, 2008. 2.

44. Rumley, Dennis (ed.). *The Indian Ocean region: Security, stability and sustainability in the 21st century*. Melbourne: Australia India Institute, 2013. 58.
45. Mensah, Thomas. 2004. "The place of the ISPS code in the legal international regime." *WMU Journal of Maritime Affairs*, Vol. 3:1. 17–18.
46. United Nations. 1982. United Nations Convention on the Law of the Sea. Available at: http://www.un.org/depts/los/convention_agreements/texts/unclos/unclos_e.pdf.
47. Grotius, Hugo. *The free sea*. Indianapolis: Liberty Fund, 2004 (originally published 1609).
48. Diaz, Leticia and Dubner, Barry. 2004. "On the problem of utilizing unilateral action to prevent acts of sea piracy and terrorism: A proactive approach to the evolution of international law." *Syracuse Journal of International Law and Commerce*, Vol. 32:1. 1–5.
49. Murphy, Martin. *Small boats, weak states, dirty money: Piracy and maritime terrorism in the modern world*. London: Hurst Publishing, 2009. 185–189.
50. Scheffler, Alessandro. *Piracy—Threat or nuisance?* Rome: Nato Defense College, 2010. 9–10.
51. Examples include: Vrey, Francois. 2009. "Bad order at sea: From the Gulf of Aden to the Gulf of Guinea." *African Security Review*, Vol. 18:3. 18–20; Kraska, J. and Pedrozo, R. A. *International maritime security law*. 16; and Brits, Pieter and Nel, Michelle. "UNCLOS and good order at Sea: A normative framework." in: Vrey, Francois, and Mandrup, Thomas (eds.) *Towards good order at sea: African experiences*. Stellenbosch: Sun Media, 2015. 51.
52. Keil, Kathrin. 2013. "The Arctic: A new region of conflict? The case of oil and gas." *Cooperation and Conflict*, Vol. 49:2. 162–190; Kirchberger, Sarah. *Assessing China's Naval Power*. Berlin: Springer, 2015.
53. Examples include: Mulqueen, Michael, Sanders, Deborah, and Speller, Ian (eds.) *Small navies: Strategy and policy for small navies in war and peace*. London: Routledge, 2014; Germond, Basil. *The maritime dimension of European security*. Basingstoke: Palgrave Macmillan, 2015; and Riddervold, Marianne. *The maritime turn in EU foreign and security policies*. Basingstoke: Palgrave Macmillan, 2018.
54. Bueger, Christian. 2015. "What is maritime security." *Marine Policy*, Vol. 53. 160.
55. African Union. 2012. *2050 Africa's integrated maritime strategy*. 8–10. Available at: https://cggrps.com/wp-content/uploads/2050-AIM-Strategy_EN.pdf.
56. Examples include: Guilfoyle, Douglas (ed.). *Modern piracy: Challenges and responses*. Cheltenham: Edward Elgar, 2013; Brits, Pieter and Nel,

Michelle. 2015. "UNCLOS and good order at sea: A normative framework", in: Mandrup, Thomas, and Very, Francois (eds.) *Towards good order at sea: African experiences.* Stellenbosch: Sun Media, 2015. 75–96.
57. Murphy, *Small boats, weak states, dirty money.* 52–53.
58. Personal interview with international oil company representative, October 2018.
59. Rigby, Ben. 2018. Africa's opportunity as a global oil and gas hub. Available at: https://www.africanlawbusiness.com/news/8318-africa-s-opportunity-as-a-global-oil-and-gas-hub.
60. Seisay, Mohamed, Sidibe, Aboubacar, and Nouala, Simplice (eds.) *Economic, social and environmental impact of illegal, unreported and unregulated fishing in Africa.* Nairobi: Interafrican Bureau for Animal Resources, 2016.
61. See, for example, Polle, Benjamin. 2016. Afrique de l'Ouest: les rouages de la pêche illégale passés au crible. Jeune Afrique. Available at: https://www.jeuneafrique.com/337407/economie/afrique-de-louest-rouages-de-peche-illegale-passes-crible/; Bagnetto, Laura Angela. 2019. Somalia: Chinese deal angers fishing communities, sparks concerns over sovereignty and piracy. RFI. Available at: http://en.rfi.fr/africa/20190207-Somalia-Chinese-deal-angers-fishing-communities-sparks-concerns-over-sovereignty-and.
62. The environmental NGO *Global Fishing Watch* (https://globalfishingwatch.org) provides good examples for the use of modern technology to track and visualise fishing activities around the globe.
63. Denmark provides a good example for the international involvement in the fight against insecurity at sea: Ministry of Foreign Affairs of Denmark. *Priority paper for the Danish efforts to combat piracy and other types of maritime crime 2019–2022.* Copenhagen: Ministry of Foreign Affairs, 2018.
64. Todd, Daniel and Lindberg, Michael. *Navies and shipbuilding industries: The strained symbiosis.* Westport: Greenwood Publishing, 1996. 56–57.

CHAPTER 3

Lubricants for Development

Abstract Two key components of the blue economy are the main focus of this chapter: maritime trade and the exploitation of offshore oil and gas reserves. Both sectors share key characteristics and are influenced by various factors. Maritime security is an important aspect when large-scale projects in either sector are planned. Considering that both maritime trade—through customs duties—and offshore oil and gas production—through taxes and royalties—offer direct revenues for governments, investments into better provision of security at sea could even lead to additional resources in the short term. These would then be available for other types of government spending, for example on unrelated issues such as health care or education. Several initiatives, notably the African Union's (AU) *2050 AIM Strategy*, underline that links between maritime security and economic factors have gained increasing recognition in recent years. That is further highlighted by planned and ongoing investments in the offshore oil and gas industry as well as into port infrastructure in both East and West Africa.

Keywords Maritime trade · Offshore oil and gas · *2050 AIM Strategy* · Government revenues

In many countries, the maritime domain has enormous economic potential. More often than not, however, this potential remains untapped. Maritime issues in general—and maritime security in particular—are not

D. Siebels, *Maritime Security in East and West Africa*,
https://doi.org/10.1007/978-3-030-22688-6_3

of great concern to the general public, to the media or to politicians.[1] Scarce resources are more likely to be used to address security issues on land, and issues at sea are rarely a political priority and may even be completely ignored without specific lobbying efforts.

This chapter highlights the economic significance of the maritime environment in East and West Africa. Calculating the blue economy's impact on GDP growth or unemployment rates is beyond the scope of this book, yet it is essential to underline that security at sea is not an end in itself. By and large, governments rarely consider maritime security issues to be of vital importance to the general population or even to regime survival. Economic reasons, however, may change this perception since additional resources created by a strengthened blue economy can then be spent on land, addressing challenges like education or health care which are immediately visible for the population as a whole.

Offshore oil and gas deposits are the prime examples for the blue economy's potential impact. Impressive growth rates for maritime trade are another aspect that may draw the attention of politicians. Both sectors are covered in this chapter while the importance of fish stocks for domestic economies is discussed in Chapter 4. In all three areas, positive economic impacts can only be maximised when security issues at sea are addressed. That requires sustainable investments in government agencies with a maritime remit, but also regional cooperation because security problems at sea are rarely limited to a single country.

Looking at the exploitation of offshore oil and gas deposits as well as maritime trade in the same chapter makes sense due to similar characteristics:

- The overall number of jobs generated directly by the offshore industry or by port operators is limited.
- Both areas have an indirect impact on economic development, for example through the domestic use of offshore gas production or better integration into global value chains via maritime trade routes.
- National governments can benefit from direct revenues, for example through customs duties collected in ports or royalties from the offshore sector.

The third aspect in particular is important as the tax base in most African countries is significantly smaller than in developed economies.[2] Other income sources are therefore vital for governments, and a lack of maritime security can have a very direct impact on revenue flows as will be shown in this chapter.

Different National Requirements

Various economic activities can be linked to the blue economy which is set to become even more important in the coming years.[3] Maritime security challenges, however, are very different on the national level.

In West Africa, offshore oil and gas production has long been established in countries like Nigeria, Gabon, Equatorial Guinea or Gabon and is set to increase further.[4] In Benin and Togo, the ports in Cotonou and Lomé are of strategic importance for the respective governments.[5] Ghana faces problems with IUU fishing,[6] but the government also wants to develop maritime trade and expand offshore oil and gas production.[7]

In East Africa, most countries suffer from IUU fishing[8] while large-scale offshore gas production is very likely to begin in the coming years in Mozambique[9] and Tanzania.[10] The tourism industry in the Seychelles and in Kenya has been badly affected by Somali piracy.[11] At the same time, countries as diverse as Djibouti,[12] Kenya[13] and even landlocked Ethiopia[14] are trying to boost maritime trade.

These are just some examples to underline that maritime security requirements are varied. Navies or coastguards may be used to protect specific offshore installations or to conduct patrols throughout the Exclusive Economic Zones (EEZ) where fishing activities have to be monitored and relevant regulations have to be enforced. These tasks require very different assets and capabilities. On the political level, outside actors may push for new laws to prosecute pirate attacks against merchant ships, yet governments might prioritise the complicated legal framework for offshore oil production instead. Finally, national requirements have to be aligned to improve regional coordination.

This chapter highlights the economic impact of maritime trade as well as offshore oil and gas production for countries in East and West Africa. Both areas provide direct revenues for governments. Investing to improve maritime security often creates significant returns, even within a relatively short period. Potential revenues can be calculated and summarised in a maritime business plan. Such a plan quantifies the benefits of better security at sea and is important as the foundation for a comprehensive maritime strategy. At the same time, this approach centres on the perspectives of stakeholders who benefit from improved maritime security as recipients, not merely on navies, coastguards or security companies as providers.[15]

3.1 Structure and Governance of Africa's Blue Economy

Governance in the maritime environment differs significantly from similar issues on land. First and foremost, there is no 'public' or 'private' ownership of offshore areas, and these are instead used for different economic activities such as fishing, oil production or merchant shipping. Territorial waters and the EEZ always remain a public good, turning any country's maritime domain into an asset that should be managed carefully. Countries throughout East and West Africa, however, have generally failed to acknowledge this potential in the past, highlighted by a '[l]ack of appropriate policy, legal and institutional frameworks for governance of the maritime zones'.[16]

Over the past decade, policymakers have finally shown an increasing interest in maritime matters, including—but not limited to—maritime security.[17] Even a basic issue such as the delimitation of maritime boundaries, however, is not a priority 'in the absence of incursions by adjacent neighbours or any incidents or natural resources'.[18] The dispute between Ghana and Côte d'Ivoire, for example, was settled by an international tribunal in 2017, but only after oil discoveries had been made in a disputed area.[19] Both countries had been independent since 1957 (Ghana) and 1960 (Côte d'Ivoire) respectively.

Failure to implement international conventions is another symptom for the lack of urgency when it comes to maritime governance. Many African countries have signed and ratified conventions such as United Nations Convention on the Law of the Sea (UNCLOS) or the International Ship and Port Facility Security (ISPS) Code. Nevertheless, domestic legislation is often patchy, making it complicated or even impossible to actually implement the respective conventions. Shortcomings in maritime expertise and a lack of political will are the main challenges, and major improvements are therefore unlikely in the short or even the medium term.[20]

Even when governments successfully address these issues, regional cooperation remains complicated. Similar to other world regions, questions of sovereignty have to be addressed. These are often exacerbated by different colonial heritages[21]—which are particularly pronounced in Africa—and personal rivalries between leading politicians. In short, it is challenging to find common ground in the maritime environment when there is no tradition of cooperation to tackle land-based security threats. That includes talks on the political level as well as the implementation of any agreed measures on the operational level.

Continental Initiatives

National and regional efforts to improve maritime security in East and West Africa should be analysed merely as a part of the maritime environment in general. As mentioned above, it is rare that security is regarded as an end in itself by governments. Other aspects, notably economic impacts, therefore have to be taken into account.

On the continental level, the African Union (AU) recognises the economic potential of the sea. In 2009, the organisation's assembly supported 'initiatives undertaken by the Commission to develop a comprehensive and coherent strategy',[22] while a conference of transport ministers led to a call on the AU to 'accelerate the implementation of various United Nations instruments relating to maritime safety, maritime security and the protection of the maritime environment'.[23] During the same conference, the *African Maritime Transport Charter* was adopted, showing that maritime transport began to gain recognition 'as a key component of an African socio-economic development policy'.[24]

In practice, however, neither the AU nor the regional economic communities across the continent had sufficient capacities to implement relevant measures and reach their newly stated goals. The AU therefore partnered with the Brenthurst Foundation, a South African think tank, and secured external funding for a project that looked at links between maritime trade and piracy. Main outcome of this project was a discussion paper which pointed out that any maritime strategy has to 'provide a coherent policy framework and contribute to the optimal development of all maritime-related activities in a sustainable manner'.[25]

Over the following years, the AU developed *2050 Africa's Integrated Maritime Strategy* (*2050 AIM Strategy*), which was officially adopted in January 2014. It seems unlikely that the lofty ambitions laid out in the strategy can be reached. It covers a 'wide variety of sectors and a complex array of institutions, initiatives and programmes',[26] leading to fragmentation in an area where a lack of financial and human resources is already a major issue. It is far from certain that national governments will follow the advice that was laid out in the Brenthurst Foundation's discussion paper already in 2010: investments to improve maritime security 'can be justified if compared to the cost of resource losses'.[27]

3.2 Offshore Oil and Gas Production

While the actual amount of oil and gas production in sub-Saharan Africa is low compared to other regions, hydrocarbons are an essential contributor to the overall GDP and to government revenues in countries where such production takes place.

Table 3.1 underlines that many governments have failed to diversify national economies, instead relying on oil rents. The World Bank defines these as 'revenues above the cost of extracting the resources'.[28] Unless oil rents are invested into new capital such as infrastructure or a sovereign wealth fund, the respective country's capital stock is liquidated over time, allowing the government to borrow against the future. Significantly lower oil rents in 2014 and 2015 were largely due to a severe drop in crude oil prices, underlined by a slight increase in 2016, the last year for which figures were available at the time of writing.

Large contributions to GDP do not directly create government revenues, yet the unbalanced relation between oil revenues and taxes is equally problematic, highlighted by the figures in Table 3.2. At the time of writing, 2014 was the most recent year for which these figures were available, but the overall picture was very similar to previous years and is unlikely to have changed significantly since, particularly after the rebound in oil prices that started in 2016.

Table 3.1 Oil rents (percentage of GDP)[a]

	2012	*2013*	*2014*	*2015*	*2016*
Republic of Congo	54.5	42.2	36.2	17.3	19.4
Equatorial Guinea	36	30.9	24.6	12.4	14.9
Angola	41.2	34.5	27.1	10.8	12.6
Gabon	37.3	31.4	24.9	9.3	10.4
Nigeria	14.3	11.1	8.5	3	3.5

[a]World Bank. 2019. Oil rents (% of GDP). Available at: https://data.worldbank.org/indicator/NY.GDP.PETR.RT.ZS?end=2016&start=2012&year_low_desc=true

Table 3.2 Public finances (percentage of GDP) for 2014[a]

	Total revenues and grants	*Tax revenues*	*Oil revenues*	*Factor oil revenue/ tax revenue*
Equatorial Guinea	38	2.7	29.8	11.04
Angola	38.4	5.9	30.8	5.22
Republic of Congo	42.7	8.5	32	3.76
Gabon	25.9	11.2	14	1.25
Cameroon	17.7	11	4.7	0.43
Ghana	21.2	15.9	0.2	0.01

[a]Organisation for Economic Co-operation and Development. 2019. *OECD.Stat*. Available at: https://stats.oecd.org/Index.aspx?DataSetCode=AEO11_COUNTRYNOTES_TAB4_EN

The most prominent example for a disproportionate level of oil revenues compared to tax revenues is Equatorial Guinea. For every dollar collected in taxes, customs duties and social security contributions—which are all covered under tax revenues—the government collected 11.04 dollars from the oil and gas industry. In Angola, the Republic of Congo and Gabon, revenues collected from oil and gas companies were also higher than the overall revenues collected through different forms of taxes, highlighting that governments are extremely reliant on this particular income stream.

All countries shown in Tables 3.1 and 3.2 are in West Africa. However, the development of large offshore gas deposits in Mozambique and Tanzania can easily lead to a similar situation in both countries.

Overall, maritime security is primarily a concern for the oil and gas industry when exploration and production take place offshore. Reliable figures about the relative amount of offshore production in different countries are not publicly available. Countries like Ghana, Equatorial Guinea or Angola rely almost exclusively on offshore production. In other countries, onshore production covers a significant proportion of the overall output, yet oil fields on land are generally mature and production is likely to decline in the short to medium term. The development of new fields takes place almost exclusively offshore. Various countries in East and West Africa are trying to ramp up or start exports of oil and gas in the coming years.[29]

Offshore operations are not necessarily limited by a lack of security at sea. Developing any offshore field requires large investments and it takes years before production can start. International oil companies are therefore able to contribute significantly to security in the vicinity of their assets. Most governments even provide military personnel as crew for security vessels which are chartered by oil companies or their suppliers and operate around specific ships and offshore installations.[30]

Situation in West Africa

Beginning in mid-2014, oil prices dropped significantly, leading virtually all oil companies to postpone many investment decisions. More recently, however, the situation has changed once again and several governments in West Africa are hoping to establish or boost offshore production in the coming years.[31] At the same time, national oil companies continue to rely on partnerships with international oil majors due to a lack of resources and expertise for the development of offshore deposits.[32]

Analysts expect '[d]ouble-digit increases in annual spending on new oil and gas projects in Africa'[33] until 2030. Several countries in West Africa, notably Angola, Nigeria and Senegal, are likely to receive a large share of these investments to expand production at existing offshore fields or to develop new deposits.[34] At the same time, the structure of the offshore industry in the three countries mentioned above is fundamentally different:

- Angola has a long-established offshore industry. After the civil war ended in 2002, activities increased significantly and virtually all oil production comes from offshore fields.[35] Protection of offshore assets and land-based infrastructure is largely provided by military personnel, yet there have been no reports of attacks against offshore facilities so far. Very few attacks against merchant ships have been reported in recent years, and the most notable incident was the hijacking of the product tanker KERALA off Luanda in January 2014.[36]
- Nigeria's oil industry started with the first commercially viable discovery in 1956. For several decades, most crude oil was produced on land and in shallow water across the Niger Delta region. In the more recent past, the percentage of offshore production has steadily increased to 44% of natural gas and 68% of crude oil production in 2017.[37] International oil companies in particular have concentrated on the offshore sector, partly motivated by security concerns on land. However, maritime security is a major concern and attacks

against merchant ships as well as offshore supply vessels are frequent off the southern and western Niger Delta.[38]

- Senegal's government hopes that the country will benefit from large offshore discoveries.[39] First exports of natural gas are expected by 2022,[40] and additional exploration activities are also ongoing. At the same time, the country's important fishing industry is already in crisis[41] and the construction of offshore facilities may lead to confrontations with artisanal fishermen, creating hitherto unknown maritime security challenges.

Terrorist attacks are often mentioned as a potential threat for the offshore sector in West Africa.[42] So far, however, no such attack in the maritime environment has been recorded throughout the region. Militant groups in Nigeria have successfully targeted facilities off the Niger Delta in the past, yet these attacks have to be analysed in the context of domestic insurgencies and have not been reported since an amnesty programme was announced in 2009.

Nevertheless, governments across the region regard facilities operated by the oil and gas industry as strategic assets which are often protected by government security forces.[43] Attacks against such assets would put economic pressure on governments, and offshore facilities therefore 'can attract the attention of criminal and political elements not because of *what* it represents, but rather because of *whom* it represents'.[44] Unique forms of cooperation between security forces, private security companies and oil majors have therefore developed across the region, underlining the need for additional investments into maritime security.

Situation in East Africa

For the oil and gas industry, East Africa has long been a so-called frontier region. There is almost no history of production in the region, neither onshore nor offshore. The discovery of large natural gas deposits off Mozambique and Tanzania has changed this situation, leading to optimistic predictions[45] and increasing interest in further exploration across a region where such activities were hampered by the threat of Somali piracy until recently.[46]

Revenues from offshore gas production are likely to have a transformative effect on national economies. Whether the impact will be positive for large parts of the population is an ongoing discussion, but some potential problems can already be identified. Fishing activities in particular are 'vulnerable to damages from oil and gas exploration',[47] increasing the need to allow for a diverse range of activities throughout any country's EEZ. Fishermen in Mozambique already had to face negative local effects of developments that may be good for the national economy: '[W]hile the influx of workers has been good for fish prices, (…) gas drilling is pushing fish farther out to sea'[48] and fishing is even banned completely in some areas.

At the same time, Mozambique's navy does not have the capacities to ensure a secure maritime environment, underlined by an agreement with neighbouring South Africa. In 2011, South African naval vessels started to patrol in the Mozambique Channel to protect the area from attacks by Somalia-based pirates.[49] In April 2018, South African President Cyril Ramaphosa approved the extension of the counter-piracy operation for another year.[50]

Both Tanzania and Mozambique started to increase naval capacities and maritime expertise overall after gas discoveries dramatically increased the economic potential of their respective EEZs. In Tanzania, the government even started to cooperate with a private security company to provide military personnel as armed guards on ships related to the offshore industry in a short-term response to immediate requirements.[51] In Mozambique, attempts to increase naval capacities were also made, although these have been marred by a wide-ranging corruption scandal.[52]

Large-scale offshore activities in East Africa have so far been limited to Mozambique and Tanzania. It is nevertheless possible that more oil and gas deposits will be found in the coming years. Favourable geography and a lack of exploration in the past offer opportunities, yet governments have also realised that maritime security issues have to be addressed to attract further interest from the private sector.

So far, additional capacities have been mainly added on the national level. Despite some initiatives, largely funded by external actors, cooperation to improve maritime security across East Africa remains hampered by various factors, analysed in more detail in the following chapters. Even if further offshore oil and gas deposits are discovered, they are unlikely to change the situation significantly because positive effects will mostly be realised by the respective countries. At the same time, even the potential impact of offshore hydrocarbons has already led to an increased interest in maritime security questions throughout the region, albeit still on a very low level compared to many other political issues.

3.3 The Critical Role of Ports

Analysing maritime trade provides important indications for economic development in a specific region or country. On the African continent, maritime trade 'is shaped by the continent's trade concentration and limited diversification'.[53] Exports comprise mainly of crude oil and other raw materials, while petroleum products and natural gas are among the main imports in many African countries.

Even though cargo volumes have increased over the past decade, growth has been much slower than in other regions around the world. Between 2006 and 2017, Africa's percentage share of worldwide maritime trade has therefore decreased in terms of goods loaded by volume (from 9.4% in 2006 to 6.8% in 2017) and remained almost steady for goods unloaded by volume (from 4.4% in 2006 to 4.7% in 2017) as shown in Fig. 3.1.[54] Over the same period, Africa's share of the world's overall population grew from 14.1 to 16.6%,[55] meaning that maritime trade on the continent has fallen further behind other world regions.

These figures indicate the potential for growth in terms of maritime trade. Better integration into global shipping routes would help to lower

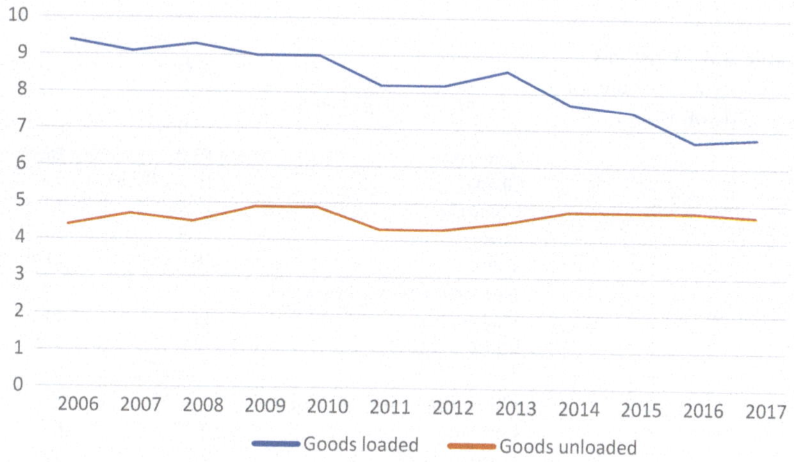

Fig. 3.1 World seaborne trade by volume 2006–2017, percentage share of Africa (United Nations Conference on Trade and Development. 2019. UNCTADstat: World seaborne trade by types of cargo and by groups of economies, annual)

transport costs, removing at least some barriers for more regional and international trade. Better infrastructure and efficient procedures are 'critical if Africa's linkages to the global economy are to be improved and economic integration within the continent is to be encouraged'.[56]

While some factors are beyond the control of any national government, others are subject to political decisions. 'Unlike distance [between ports], port efficiency can be influenced by policymakers',[57] creating a more favourable environment for the private sector. Maritime transport will also play a crucial role in the African Continental Free Trade Area, established in March 2018.[58]

Economists generally agree that free trade will boost regional trade and, by extension, economic growth. At the same time, customs duties are an important source of income for governments across sub-Saharan Africa, representing a much larger portion of overall government revenues than in developed economies, shown in Table 3.3.

Joining a free trade agreement is likely to have at least some impact on government budgets. The tax base in countries across East and West Africa is relatively small, whereas customs duties can easily be collected at the point of entry. By and large, the vast majority of customs duties are

Table 3.3 Customs duties in tax revenue for selected countries in %[a]

	2016	*2017*
West Africa (selected countries)		
Benin	16.9	16.9
Cameroon	14.3	15.2
Ghana	16.2 (2015)	n.a.
Guinea	19.1	22.9
Senegal	13.1	13.7
Togo	20.3	21.8
East Africa (selected countries)		
Madagascar	11.3	11.3
Mozambique	7.4	0.8
Tanzania	7.2 (2015)	n.a.
Comparison (selected countries)		
Germany	0.8	0.8
Japan	1.7	1.6
United States	1	1

[a]World Customs Organization. *Annual Reports 2018, 2017 and 2016*. Available at: http://www.wcoomd.org/en/about-us/what-is-the-wco/annual-reports.aspx

therefore collected in ports, meaning that they are vital hubs in terms of direct revenues for governments.

At the same time, the performance of customs agencies is rarely measured in terms of efficiency, and collection of revenues is a much more important factor. That provides the respective agencies with significantly more political leverage than in developed countries. Any reform attempt may therefore lead to additional political implications. Moreover, not even high-ranking customs officers may have the power to conduct reforms within their own organisations where 'corruption and bad practices induce a strong asymmetry of information between the head of administration and their grassroots officials who are, on the field, in charge of applying the new procedures during a reform process'.[59]

On the face of it, inefficient infrastructure and cumbersome customs procedures are not security problems. However, these issues are inextricably linked with congestion in ports, forcing ships to wait at anchor where they may be targeted by attackers. At the same time, African governments have to expand ports as well as 'streamline maritime bureaucratic procedures and improve maritime security'[60] to strengthen economic growth and development. Limited security at sea puts a strain on maritime trade, '[p]orts reputedly vulnerable and located in high risk areas will likely suffer from profit margin erosion resulting from a loss in traffic, overcapacity and high operating costs'.[61] In short, maritime security is an important selling point for port administrations and should therefore be included in the strategic development plan of any port across East and West Africa.

Situation in West Africa

During the colonial period, ports were by and large needed to collect raw materials produced in the hinterland for shipments to the respective colonial power. Transport infrastructure was built based on those requirements, and major roads or railroads did not cut across colonial boundaries. This colonial heritage led to the development of many relatively small ports throughout the region which were regarded as important parts of the national infrastructure by virtually all governments after independence,[62] limiting economies of scale and keeping transport costs high.

The lack of maritime security has been another long-standing problem for West Africa. The International Maritime Organization's (IMO) first piracy-related resolution was issued in the early 1980s, specifically concerned with the region. 'The high incidence of piracy and armed robbery in certain notorious areas of the world, particularly around West Africa has caused great embarrassment to governments in these areas, and has increased the reluctance of some shipping lines to operate along their coasts',[63] seafarers' unions even called for a boycott of vessels calling at ports in West Africa.

Cotonou in Benin provides a more recent example for the potential impact of a lack of security at sea. When Nigerian security forces increasingly targeted criminal activities in the maritime environment in early 2011, some of these activities were merely displaced across the maritime border between both countries. Between March and September 2011, ten ships carrying petroleum products were hijacked off Cotonou. All of these vessels were less than 70 nautical miles away from the coastline, and some were even attacked in the immediate vicinity of the port (Fig. 3.2).

The spate of attacks led to fewer port calls in Cotonou. Ships were redirected to Lomé in neighbouring Togo or to Ghana's main port in Tema. Reliable figures showing the decline in maritime traffic, however, are not available. At a conference in 2011, one speaker talked about a

Fig. 3.2 Hijackings off product tankers in 2011 off Cotonou and Lagos (Risk Intelligence. 2019. Map from the *Risk Intelligence System*, a comprehensive and subscription-based online portal that includes information about maritime security incidents worldwide)

decrease of 70% in shipping activities.[64] This figure has been widely quoted since, yet local agents who are familiar with day-to-day operations in the port believe that a decline between 10 and 20% is a more accurate estimate. Based on port authority data, one study has found that 1073 ships called at Cotonou in 2012, compared with 1245 ships in 2010, representing a decline of around 14%.[65]

Benin's government nevertheless realised that any decline in maritime traffic could have an immediate impact on customs revenues and the national economy which is heavily reliant on maritime trade. On the operational level, joint patrols with the Nigerian navy started in September 2011. On the political level, the situation was even brought to the attention of the UN Security Council, analysed in more detail below.

On the other hand, failing to address maritime security challenges—including root causes—may even exacerbate the problem. Large-scale investments into offshore facilities and port infrastructure, coupled with growing populations and economic development, are very likely to lead to increasing maritime traffic across the region. Privatisation of specific terminals has also put pressure on governments to act. Private operators seek to attract as many ships as possible to secure a return on their investments. Some examples for port infrastructure that has been built or planned in recent years include:

- In Togo, a new container terminal was inaugurated in late 2014, increasing the capacity of the port to 2.2 million TEU per year. The US$380 million project was the largest infrastructure investment in the country's history, representing almost ten per cent of Togo's annual GDP.[66]
- In Côte d'Ivoire, investments of more than US$1.4 billion will significantly expand the capacity of the existing port facilities in Abidjan. Dredging of the Vridi Canal means that the port is already able to receive larger ships than before, a second container terminal is scheduled to open in 2020.[67]
- In Ghana, a new container terminal will bring the capacity of the port to more than 3.5 million TEU per year. Construction on the US$1.5 billion project started in 2016, and the terminal is scheduled to become operational in two phases in 2019 and 2020 respectively.[68]
- In Cameroon, the country's first deepwater port near Kribi was officially opened in 2018. The first two stages of the project are

supposed to cost around US$1.3 billion, although additional infrastructure is needed to link the port to Douala and Yaoundé, Cameroon's two largest cities.[69]

Other countries in West Africa also have ambitious plans for expansion of existing port facilities or even for completely new ports which are supposed to boost domestic economies. Some of the most important examples for the latter category can be found in the Democratic Republic of Congo (Port of Banana),[70] Nigeria (Lekki and Badagry) and Senegal (Port de Futur).[71]

Together with some smaller ongoing and planned projects, these examples show that governments across West Africa are desperate to address investment requirements that have built up over time. Better port infrastructure, improved hinterland connections and reforms of administrative processes will help to lower transport costs and to stimulate maritime trade. Maritime security is one aspect that should be considered in the course of such projects. It will be easier to attract shipping companies if they are able to operate their ships in a secure environment without the need for additional protection measures. The current situation with frequent attacks against merchant vessels, particularly off Nigeria and neighbouring countries, 'negatively impacts the economic potential'[72] across the region.

Situation in East Africa

Some ports in East Africa have origins that can be traced back to ancient trading routes across the Indian Ocean,[73] yet the current infrastructure has been mainly shaped by colonial influences. Similar to West Africa, road and rail links were built from ports to the hinterland, not across colonial borders.[74] When former colonies in East Africa became independent countries, the situation remained similar due to a lack of resources and other political priorities.

The limited focus on maritime issues in general also meant that maritime security had never been perceived as an important problem in East Africa. The situation only started to change when the number of attacks by Somali pirates started to increase from 2007 onwards. Shipping companies added charges for port calls in East Africa due to the high threat level and a corresponding increase in insurance premiums. The tourism industry was also affected because most port visits by cruise ships were cancelled.

Maritime security therefore gained at least some importance for policymakers, albeit with a narrow focus on counter-piracy operations. From the beginning, these were led by international naval forces, and countries from the region only played a minor role. That was underlined by the adoption of the *Djibouti Code of Conduct* (DCoC) in 2009 which will be analysed in detail below. In short, the negative impact of Somali piracy on maritime trade was an issue, yet governments in Europe, Asia and North America were much more concerned than those in East Africa by the threat of piracy close to one of the most important shipping lanes in the world.

More recently, however, maritime security has developed into an increasingly important topic for several reasons. Some of those will be discussed in the following chapters, but several large infrastructure projects have played a major role for political discussions on the national level:

- In Tanzania, construction in the port of Dar es Salaam started in 2017, aiming to double the capacity to 28 million tonnes of cargo per year. The US$690 million project is scheduled to be finished by 2020.[75] Moreover, the government has ambitious plans to build Africa's largest container port in Bagamoyo. Financing for the US$10 billion project is supposed to be provided mainly by partners from China and Oman.[76]
- In Kenya, container-handling capacity in the port of Mombasa was increased from 1.1 to 1.7 million TEU in 2016 and will be increased further to 2.1 million TEU by 2021 at a combined cost of around $630 million. In Lamu, a completely new port is under construction with the first ship scheduled to berth by November 2019. The port is supposed to be the maritime gateway to the LAPSSET corridor, a US$30 billion infrastructure project linking northern Kenya with South Sudan and Ethiopia.[77]
- In Sudan, the government signed a US$4 billion agreement with the government of Qatar in 2018, aimed at developing the port of Suakin on the Red Sea.[78] In a separate agreement, the Turkish government announced the intention to develop the former Ottoman city into a tourism hub, causing concern in other Red Sea countries due to Suakin's strategic location.[79]

Several other projects to expand port capacities have also been announced or started, for example in Madagascar (Toamasina),[80] Mauritius (Port Louis)[81] and Eritrea (Bay of Anfile).[82] Taken together, these are good examples for an increasing awareness of maritime issues and the blue economy's potential to improve the lives of ordinary citizens.

Some of the investments mentioned above are at least somewhat inspired by strategic decisions. Nevertheless, the projects also provide commercial opportunities for all partners involved. Similar to West Africa, insecurity at sea makes it harder to attract shipping companies to ports across the region, limiting the positive effects on national economies. Governments therefore have another incentive to cooperate in an area that has traditionally received very little political attention.

3.4 Summary

Awareness for the economic potential of the sea is increasing among politicians and the general public in East and West Africa, supported by ongoing and planned investments in the offshore oil and gas sector and into port infrastructure. This new focus on the blue economy makes investments into maritime security more likely, especially when these investments have a direct and almost immediate impact on government revenues.

At the same time, maritime security remains relatively low on the list of political priorities. Governments across both East and West Africa have to address many issues that require more attention, at least in the short term. When money is spent on health care, education or energy infrastructure, results are immediately visible for the general population. Maritime security, on the other hand, requires a broader and often longer-term perspective. Moreover, a lack of security at sea is largely invisible for most people, unless they are directly affected, for example as seafarers or fishermen.

Decisions to exploit offshore oil and gas deposits require long-term investments, similar to the construction of infrastructure in and around ports. It is often impossible to quantify the impact of insecurity at sea on the economic viability of such projects. At the same time, '[a] viable maritime security program is good business'[83] when national governments consider the long-term benefits in the form of direct revenues and general economic development.

On the operational level, the provision of maritime security in the vicinity of ports or around offshore installations is similar in nature. Naval assets are only needed in specific areas or on certain routes between ports and offshore fields. Limited capacities are therefore necessary, for example small patrol boats and the ability to quickly respond to incidents. For any navy with a limited budget, a cost-benefit analysis is likely to show that additional capabilities such as comprehensive surveillance of the respective country's EEZ will not provide a good return on the required investment. Developing such capabilities is therefore not a strategic priority.

Significant differences between the offshore industry in East and West Africa can be identified in the scope of projects. In West Africa, offshore oil and gas production has been established for many years and crude oil production plays a much larger role than natural gas. In East Africa, the offshore industry cannot rely on established hub ports or supply chains, extending the timeline for the exploitation of the first commercially valid offshore deposits. Furthermore, producing and exporting natural gas requires even larger upfront investments than crude oil due to the required infrastructure to liquefy the gas before it can be loaded on ships. The costs for security provision are therefore almost negligible in comparison with the overall expenditures for the construction and operation of all required facilities.

In terms of maritime trade, the main difference between East and West Africa is the number of important ports which is directly linked to the sheer number of coastal countries between Senegal in the north and Angola in the south. The corridor between Abidjan and Lagos in particular includes several large port facilities where further growth is expected in the coming years. On the eastern side of the continent, there are few countries with comparatively long coastlines, relying on a small number of ports. At the same time, these are located close to one of the most important shipping lanes worldwide, leading from the Suez Canal through the Red Sea and the Gulf of Aden to Asia.

An adequate level of maritime security particularly around ports and on important shipping routes will be important for the commercial success of those infrastructure upgrades outlined above. Private terminal operators should use their leverage to devise comprehensive security strategies for ports, important to attract more traffic and therefore increase cargo throughput and revenues.

Benin's main port Cotonou provides a practical example. In December 2017, it was announced that the Antwerp Port Authority's consulting subsidiary Port of Antwerp International (PAI) was selected to improve port operations in Cotonou.[84] Only a few weeks after PAI took over the management of the port, two product tankers were hijacked at the Cotonou anchorage. In cooperation with the navy, the privately managed port authority then announced several measures to improve security at the anchorage, trying to ensure shipping companies that port calls in Cotonou are not a major security threat.[85]

On a more general level, unique forms of cooperation between governments and the private sector may be required to provide security around ports or for offshore assets. Throughout East and West Africa, navies and other security agencies with a maritime remit generally lack assets, funding and expertise and are therefore unable to fulfil similar mandates as, for example, naval forces in European countries. Due to the state's monopoly on the provision of security, however, such cooperation is likely to be controversial, discussed in more detail in the following chapters.

Notes

1. Dewar, Bob. 2016. On African coastlines, prosperity and security go together. *Chatham House*. Available at: https://www.chathamhouse.org/expert/comment/african-coastlines-prosperity-and-security-go-together#.
2. Ebeke, Christian, and Ehrhart, Hélène. 2011. "Tax revenue instability in sub-Saharan Africa: Consequences and remedies." *HAL*. Available at: https://halshs.archives-ouvertes.fr/halshs-00552230/document, accessed 31 January 2017. 3–7.
3. Hassan, Adam Abdou. 2016. Économie bleue en Afrique: des resource naturelles très disputées. *The Conversation*. Available at: https://theconversation.com/economie-bleue-en-afrique-des-ressources-naturelles-tres-disputees-59506.
4. Oni, Dolapo. 2018. West Africa–ready to blossom. *Petroleum Economist*. Available at: https://www.petroleum-economist.com/articles/upstream/exploration-production/2018/west-africa-ready-to-blossom.
5. For Togo, see Gnoufougou, Doman. 2013. "A causal relationship between trade and GDP growth in Togo." *International Journal of Trends in Economics, Management and Technology*, Vol. 2:4. 66–71. For Benin, see Blédé, Barthelemy. *Benin's maritime security challenges in the Gulf of Guinea*. Dakar: Institute for Security Studies, 2015.
6. See, for example, Environmental Justice Foundation and Hen Mpoano. 2019. Securing equitable and sustainable fisheries. *Report under the Far Dwuma Nkodo (Securing Sustainable Fisheries) project*. Available at: https://ejfoundation.org//resources/downloads/EJF-Ghana-transparency-position-paper-HM-final.pdf.

7. Ghana News Agency. 2019. Ghana's oil production to go up to 500,000 barrels. Available at: http://www.ghananewsagency.org/economics/ghana-s-oil-production-to-go-up-to-500-000-barrels-minister-145396.
8. Bryce, Emma. 2016. These East African countries show how teamwork and technology can thwart illegal fishing. *Ensia*. Available at: https://ensia.com/features/east-africa-illegal-ocean-fishing/.
9. Crooks, Ed. 2018. Mozambique to become a gas supplier to world. *Financial Times*. Available at: https://www.ft.com/content/d34685b2-7995-11e8-bc55-50daf11b720d.
10. Adomaitis, Nerijus. 2018. Norway's Equinor to start talks with Tanzania over LNG project. *Reuters*. Available at: https://www.reuters.com/article/us-equinor-tanzania-lng/norways-equinor-to-start-talks-with-tanzania-over-lng-project-idUSKBN1O30UC.
11. See, for example, Akwiri, Joseph. 2015. Kenya to build cruise ship terminal at its biggest port. *Reuters*. Available at: https://www.reuters.com/article/kenya-ports-tourism/kenya-to-build-cruise-ship-terminal-at-its-biggest-port-idUSL1N13D0GJ20151118#CvlSgmq5QLYaa7PV.97; World Bank. *The pirates of Somalia: ending the threat, rebuilding a nation*. Washington: The World Bank, 2013. 35–56.
12. Valentine, Harry. 2018. Port of Djibouti as a future African trading gateway. *Maritime Executive*. Available at: https://www.maritime-executive.com/editorials/port-of-djibouti-as-a-future-african-trading-gateway.
13. Murathie, Eunice. 2018. Training plan to boost maritime sector growth. *Business Daily*. Available at: https://www.businessdailyafrica.com/corporate/shipping/Training-plan-to-boost-maritime-sector-growth/4003122-4788470-e0w735z/index.html.
14. Cannon, Brendan J., and Rossiter, Ash. 2018. How an Ethiopia-backed port is changing power dynamics in the Horn of Africa. *The Conversation*. Available at: https://theconversation.com/how-an-ethiopia-backed-port-is-changing-power-dynamics-in-the-horn-of-africa-93308.
15. See also Trelawny, Chris. 2013. "Maritime security beyond military operations." *RUSI Journal*, Vol. 158:1. 48–52.
16. Wambua, Paul Musili. 2009. "Enhancing regional maritime cooperation in Africa: The planned end state." *African Security Review*, Vol. 18:3. 48.
17. Siebels, Dirk. 2017. African states don't prioritise maritime security—Here's why they should. *The Conversation*. Available at: https://theconversation.com/african-states-dont-prioritise-maritime-security-heres-why-they-should-77685.
18. Okonkwo, Theodore. 2017. "Maritime boundaries delimitation and dispute resolution in Africa". *Beijing Law Review*. Vol. 8:1. 57.
19. Farge, Emma and Kpodo, Kwasi. 2017. Court ruling favours Ghana in ocean border dispute with Ivory Coast. *Reuters*. Available at: https://

www.reuters.com/article/us-ghana-ivorycoast-boundary/court-ruling-favors-ghana-in-ocean-border-dispute-with-ivory-coast-idUSKCN-1BY0G0.
20. Personal interview with representative from the Liberia Maritime Authority, October 2015.
21. For rivalries and institutional differences between, for example, francophone and anglophone countries, see Dumbuya (2008) and Bagayoko (2012).
22. African Union. 2009. "Decision on the report of the Peace and Security Council on its activities and the state of peace and security in Africa," Assembly/AU/Dec.252(XII). Available at: http://www.peaceau.org/uploads/assembly-au-dec-252-xiii-e.pdf. 5.
23. African Union. 2009. "Durban resolution on maritime safety, maritime security and protection of the marine environment." Available at: https://www.au.int/web/sites/default/files/documents/30853-doc-durban_resolution_1.pdf. 4.
24. Economic Commission for Africa. *Assessing regional integration in Africa IV: Enhancing Intra-African Trade.* Addis Ababa: African Union, 2010. 339.
25. Brenthurst Foundation. *Maritime development in Africa—An independent specialists' framework.* Johannesburg: Brenthurst Foundation, 2010. 10.
26. Benkenstein, Alex. *Aligning Africa's maritime ambitions with broader Indian Ocean regionalism.* Johannesburg: SAIIA, 2015. 3.
27. Brenthurst Foundation. *Maritime Development in Africa.* 8.
28. World Bank. Oil rents (% of GDP).
29. For West Africa, see Walzel, Brian. 2019. New Year signals new potential in West Africa. *E&P Hart Energy.* Available at: https://www.epmag.com/new-year-signals-new-potential-west-africa-1729871. For East Africa, see: Amanam, Usua U. *Natural gas in East Africa: Domestic and regional use.* Stanford: The Stanford Natural Gas Initiative, 2017. Available at: https://ngi.stanford.edu/sites/default/files/NGI_EAfrica_LitReview%284-17%29.pdf.
30. Personal interview with representative from international oil company, March 2019.
31. Walzel, Brian. 2019. New Year signals new potential in West Africa. *Hart Energy.* Available at: https://www.hartenergy.com/exclusives/new-year-signals-new-potential-west-africa-177256.
32. PricewaterhouseCoopers. 2018. *Taking on tomorrow: Africa oil & gas review.* Available at: https://www.pwc.co.za/en/assets/pdf/africa-oil-and-gas-review-2018.pdf.
33. Fraser, John. 2018. Africa on brink of upstream surge. *Natural Gas World.* Available at: https://www.naturalgasworld.com/africa-on-brink-of-upstream-surge-ngw-magazine-66036.

34. PricewaterhouseCoopers. *Taking on tomorrow*.
35. Deloitte. 2018. *Africa oil & gas state of play*. Available at: https://www2.deloitte.com/content/dam/Deloitte/xe/Documents/energy-resources/africa_oil_gas_state_of_play_Nov2018.pdf. 12–14.
36. Slavina, Svitlana. 2014. "Tanker KERALA hijacking is on investigation." *FleetMon*. Available at: https://www.fleetmon.com/maritime-news/2014/3098/tanker-kerala-hijacking-investigation/.
37. Deloitte. *Africa oil & gas state of play*.
38. Personal interview with maritime security analyst, January 2019.
39. Ward, Andrew. 2018. Discoveries in Senegal focus attention on avoiding the 'oil curse'. *Financial Times*. Available at: https://www.ft.com/content/d979a1e0-2ea8-11e8-97ec-4bd3494d5f14.
40. Oirere, Shem. 2018. Momentum building offshore Senegal. *Offshore Engineer*. Available at: https://www.oedigital.com/news/461011-momentum-building-offshore-senegal.
41. Beatley, Meaghan, and Edwards, Sam. 2018. Overfished: In Senegal, empty nets lead to hunger and violence. *GlobalPost Investigations*. Available at: https://gpinvestigations.pri.org/overfished-in-senegal-empty-nets-lead-to-hunger-and-violence-e3b5d0c9a686.
42. For example, Onuoha, Freedom C. *Piracy and maritime security in the Gulf of Guinea: Nigeria as a microcosm*. Doha: Al Jazeera Centre for Studies, 2012: 4; Kyrou, Christos, and Wallace, Kaade. 2014. The Gulf of Guinea: Maritime Piracy's New Global Nerve Center. *Fair Observer*. Available at: https://www.fairobserver.com/region/middle_east_north_africa/gulf-guinea-maritime-piracys-global-nerve-center-18429/.
43. Personal interview with representative from international oil company, March 2019.
44. Hawkes, Roger. "Securing the offshore oil industry in the Gulf of Guinea." 143, in: Berube, Claude, and Cullen, Patrick (eds.) *Maritime private security—Market responses to piracy, terrorism and waterborne security risks in the 21st century*. London: Routledge, 2012. 138–149.
45. Crooks, Ed. 2018. Mozambique to become a gas supplier to world. Available at: https://www.ft.com/content/d34685b2-7995-11e8-bc55-50daf11b720d.
46. Stoddard, Ed. 2016. Prospect of offshore oil offers mixed blessings for Somalia. *Reuters*. Available at: https://www.reuters.com/article/us-africa-oil-somalia/prospect-of-offshore-oil-offers-mixed-blessing-for-somalia-idUSKBN1321IW.
47. Nazerali, Sean. *Improving the quality, capacity and compliance of environmental licensing processes in Mozambique: The case of the oil and gas industry*. Johannesburg: SAIIA, 2014. 5.

48. Maylie, Devon, and Gilbert, Daniel. 2014. Anadarko's controversial Mozambique project shows appetite for natural gas. *Wall Street Journal.* Available at: https://www.wsj.com/articles/anadarkos-controversial-mozambique-project-shows-appetite-for-natural-gas-1407810602.
49. Martin, Guy. 2014. Operation Copper now only with SA and Mozambique. *Defence Web.* Available at: https://www.defenceweb.co.za/security/maritime-security/operation-copper-now-only-with-sa-and-mozambique/?catid=108%3Amaritime-security.
50. No author. 2018. Ramaphosa approves Op Copper extension. *DefenceWeb.* Available at: https://www.defenceweb.co.za/security/maritime-security/ramaphosa-approves-op-copper-extension/.
51. Husband, Laura. 2013. High risk, high reward: talking offshore oil security with Drum Cussac. *Offshore Technology.* Available at: https://www.offshore-technology.com/features/featureoffshore-oil-security-piracy-terrorist-attack-prevention-drum-cussac/.
52. Cotterill, Joseph. 2019. Mozambique's ruling party closes ranks over 'tuna bond' scandal. *Financial Times.* Available at: https://www.ft.com/content/4c7e8b30-15ab-11e9-a581-4ff78404524e.
53. United Nations Conference on Trade and Development. 2018. Maritime trade and Africa. *Press Release.* Available at: https://unctad.org/en/pages/PressRelease.aspx?OriginalVersionID=476.
54. These figures are not available for sub-Saharan Africa only and therefore include countries in northern Africa as well.
55. Population Reference Bureau. *2006 world population data sheet.* Washington: Population Reference Bureau, 2006, and *2017 world population data sheet.* Washington: Population Reference Bureau, 2017. Available at: https://www.prb.org/wp-content/uploads/2006/08/06WorldDataSheet.pdf, and https://www.prb.org/wp-content/uploads/2017/08/WPDS-2017.pdf.
56. Jones, Russel, and Viros, Camille. 2014. Foundations for growth—Infrastructure investment in emerging markets. *Trafigura White Paper.* 25. Available at: https://www.trafigura.com/media/2359/traf2429_14_llewellyn_infrastructure_paper_sp_lr.pdf.
57. United Nations Conference on Trade and Development. *Review of maritime transport 2015.* New York and Geneva: United Nations, 2015. 54.
58. Signé, Landry. 2018. Why Africa's free trade area offers so much promise. *The Conversation.* Available at: https://theconversation.com/why-africas-free-trade-area-offers-so-much-promise-93827.
59. Cantens, Raballand and Djeuwo. *Cameroon Customs reform: 'gazing into the mirror'.* Paris: Organisation for Economic Co-operation and Development, 2011. 1.

60. Ncube, Mthuli, and Baker, Michael Lyon. 2011. "Beyond pirates and drugs: Unlocking Africa's maritime potential and economic development." *African Security Review*, Vol. 20:1. 64.
61. United Nations Conference on Trade and Development. *Maritime Piracy—Part I: An overview of trends, costs and trade-related implications.* New York and Geneva: United Nations, 2014. 22.
62. Debrie, Jean. 2012. "The West African port system: Global insertion and regional particularities." In: *EchoGéo*, No. 20. 3.
63. International Maritime Bureau. *A third report into the incidence of piracy and armed robbery from merchant ships.* London: International Maritime Bureau, 1985. 6.
64. Hayduk, Daniel. 2011. Joining forces to fight piracy in the Gulf of Guinea. *The New Humanitarian*. Available at: http://www.thenewhumanitarian.org/news/2011/11/29/joining-forces-fight-piracy-gulf-guinea.
65. Blédé, Barthelemy. *Benin's maritime security challenges in the Gulf of Guinea*. Dakar: Institute for Security Studies, 2015. 6–7.
66. Rogers, David. 2017. Africa's port revolution: West Coast to welcome the world. *Global Construction Review*. Available at: http://www.globalconstructionreview.com/sectors/africas-ports-revolution-w7est-coa7st-welc7ome/.
67. Kobri, Borgia, and Dosso, Zeinab. 2019. Côte d'Ivoire: $1.4 billion to be invested in Abidjan port by 2020. *Ecofin Agency*. Available at: https://www.ecofinagency.com/public-management/2802-39733-cote-d-ivoire-1-4-billion-to-be-invested-in-abidjan-port-by-2020.
68. Afenu, Sandra Esinam. 2019. First phase of Tema port expansion project to be operational in June. *Joy Online*. Available at: https://www.myjoyonline.com/business/2019/february-25th/first-phase-of-tema-port-expansion-project-to-be-operational-in-june.php.
69. Bax, Pauline. 2018. Chinese-built port evokes dreams of El Dorado in Cameroon. *Bloomberg*. Available at: https://www.bloomberg.com/news/features/2018-08-29/china-stakes-its-claim-on-west-africa.
70. Wee, Vincent. 2018. DP World wins 30-year concession for Port of Banana in Democratic Republic of the Congo. *Seatrade*. Available at: http://www.seatrade-maritime.com/news/middle-east-africa/dp-world-wins-30-year-for-port-of-banana-in-democratic-republic-of-the-congo.html.
71. Rogers, David. 2017. Africa's port revolution: West Coast to welcome the world.
72. Larsen, Jakob Paaske. 2019. EU, China and the USA need to support counter-piracy operations in the Gulf of Guinea. *BIMCO*. Available at: https://www.bimco.org/news/priority-news/20190108-call-for-gog-counter-piracy.

73. Phillips, Andrew, and Sharman, J. C. *International order in diversity: War, trade and rule in the Indian Ocean*. Cambridge: Cambridge University Press, 2015. 67–101.
74. Kavashe, Rita. 2015. Colonial boundaries continue to stifle intra-Africa trade. *The East African*. Available at: https://www.theeastafrican.co.ke/OpEd/comment/Colonial-boundaries-continue-to-stifle-intra-Africa-trade-/-/434750/2859848/-/ts9y54z/-/index.html.
75. Oirere, Shem. 2017. Grand plan—Dar es Salaam starts port expansion. *Fairplay*. Available at: https://fairplay.ihs.com/dredging/article/4293576/grand-plan-dar-es-salaam-starts-port-expansion.
76. Servant, Jean-Christophe. 2019. Will a new port make Tanzania 'Africa's Dubai'? *The Nation*. Available at: https://www.thenation.com/article/tanzania-china-bagamoyo-port/.
77. Kazungu, Kalume. 2019. First ship set to dock at Lamu berth in November. *Daily Nation*. Available at: https://www.nation.co.ke/business/First-ship-set-to-dock-at-Lamu-berth-in-November/996-4971860-2tc5q8/index.html.
78. Dudley, Dominic. 2018. East Africa becomes a testing ground for UAE and Qatar as they battle for influence and opportunity. *Forbes*. Available at: https://www.forbes.com/sites/dominicdudley/2018/04/04/uae-qatar-horn-of-africa-proxy-dispute/#316cb5366ad2.
79. Amin, Mohammed. 2018. Suakin: ‚Forgotten' Sudanese island becomes focus for Red Sea rivalries. *Middle East Eye*. Available at: https://www.middleeasteye.net/news/suakin-forgotten-sudanese-island-becomes-focus-red-sea-rivalries.
80. Japan International Cooperation Agency. 2018. Japanese ODA loan for the Toamasina port development project: Long-expected groundbreaking ceremony held in Madagascar. Available at: https://www.jica.go.jp/english/news/press/2018/180427_05.html.
81. Oirere, Shem. Port Louis expansion project aims for pre-eminence. *Fairplay*. Available at: https://fairplay.ihs.com/dredging/article/4280991/port-louis-expansion-project-aims-for-pre-eminence.
82. Manek, Nizar. 2018. Eritrea mulls port as Ethiopia rapprochement spurs investors. *Bloomberg*. Available at: https://www.bloomberg.com/news/articles/2018-08-23/eritrea-mulls-new-port-as-ethiopia-rapprochement-spurs-investors.
83. Alexander, Yonah, and Richardson, Tyler B. *Terror on the High Seas—From piracy to strategic challenge*. Santa Barbara: ABC-Clio, 2009. 268.
84. Gillis, Chris. 2017. Antwerp Port Authority picked to modernize Benin's port. *American Shipper*. Available at: https://www.americanshipper.com/news/?autonumber=70119&source=redirected-from-old-site-link.
85. Personal interview with representative from Benin's navy, November 2018.

CHAPTER 4

A Victimless Crime

Abstract In this chapter, the value of fish stocks for countries in East and West Africa and the devastating impacts of illegal, unreported and unregulated (IUU) fishing are covered. From an economic perspective, fish stocks are relevant because they provide a vital source of income for coastal communities where artisanal fishing is often one of very few employment opportunities. Moreover, well-managed stocks boost food security. In most countries throughout the regions covered in this book, per capita consumption of fish is above the world average. At the same time, IUU fishing has been an enduring problem in both regions, primarily conducted by industrial fishing vessels registered to or owned by foreign companies. Enforcement of relevant laws and regulations is problematic due to numerous factors, including a lack of naval assets and corrupt officials. A growing amount of research related to problems caused by IUU fishing has been published over the past decade. Today, it is increasingly recognised as a key aspect of maritime security, rather than merely as an environmental issue.

Keywords IUU · Artisanal fishing · Coastal communities · Law enforcement · Food security

This chapter looks at economic activities at sea that are very different from those analysed in the previous chapter. In most of the countries covered in this book, fishing is conducted both by artisanal fishermen

D. Siebels, *Maritime Security in East and West Africa*,
https://doi.org/10.1007/978-3-030-22688-6_4

from coastal communities as well as by crews on large fishing vessels, often owned by companies registered in Asian or European countries. For the former group, fishing is often the only opportunity to earn an income. The latter group may try to exploit unprotected resources simply to maximise profits. At the same time, fish stocks that are managed in a sustainable manner are a 'gift that keeps on giving'—a self-replenishing natural resource for coastal countries.

The protection of fish stocks has long been a low priority for governments and, by extension, navies, coastguards and other security agencies. In recent years, however, practitioners and academics alike have increasingly pointed out that it is indeed a security concern, not merely an environmental issue.[1] Furthermore, fishing grounds can often be found in areas used by the offshore industry or merchant ships. Conflicts of interest are therefore common and fishing operations may be perceived as security threats by seafarers on merchant vessels, simply due to a lack of knowledge about regular patterns of common fishing activities.

For many countries in East and West Africa, fish stocks are vital assets, but their economic value is very different from offshore hydrocarbons or maritime trade routes:

- Direct government revenues are limited, even in countries with a comprehensive licensing regime that is strictly enforced by relevant agencies.
- The artisanal fishing sector is one of the few sources or even the only source for employment opportunities in most coastal communities.
- Well-managed fish stocks increase food security and can help to feed a growing population.

Links between fishing and maritime security are also multifaceted. Some of the most important aspects in this regard are pointed out in this chapter.

Definitions and Economic Impacts

Uncontrolled activities of fishing vessels are often covered by the general term 'illegal fishing',[2] yet that is not a thorough description. The United Nations' Food and Agriculture Organisation (FAO) provides a technical definition that includes illegal, unreported and unregulated

(IUU) fishing as separate parts.[3] In short, unreported fishing may not be illegal because fishing vessels may have the required licence but then fail to report actual catch data. Unregulated fishing does not contravene any laws or regulations, yet catch data are unlikely to be reported correctly or at all. Any combination of these aspects makes it virtually impossible for scientists to establish sustainable catch levels for different species.

Distinguishing between legal and IUU fishing is often complicated. Crews on fishing vessels may fail to provide complete catch data to the relevant authorities or discard bycatch at sea without reporting it, even though they are licensed to operate in a specific area where they can operate legally. Such problems are likely to be worsened by a lack of oversight, yet even developed countries with comprehensive licensing regimes often use estimates rather than actual catch data as baseline for the determination of sustainable catch quotas.[4]

Overall, it is impossible to find precise figures for the extent of IUU fishing, largely due to the very nature of the problem. Scientific estimates and trade figures have been used to gain insights into the fishing sector. Fieldwork is another tool, yet such projects are expensive and therefore limited to certain areas or countries. Local fishermen may also provide anecdotal evidence which is helpful to establish a general picture, yet they are unlikely to provide verifiable data. Research about IUU fishing is further hampered by other factors, for example sales of fish products on the black market, limited recording of bycatch or a general lack of knowledge about the marine environment in a specific area.[5]

Various estimates for the extent of IUU fishing have been published in recent years, either covering the global level or the extent of the problem in certain regions. One often-quoted article[6] assesses the amount of worldwide losses caused by IUU fishing at 11 to 26 million tonnes of fish or between US$10 and 23.5 billion per year, highlighting the uncertainties that are inherent in such estimates. Moreover, the article is based on data gathered between 1980 and 2003 and does not even include catches by artisanal fishermen in the 50 countries covered by the research.[7]

Another more recent academic article includes even more alarming figures, estimating that just six countries in West Africa (Mauritania, Senegal, The Gambia, Guinea, Guinea-Bissau and Sierra Leone) lose an estimated US$2.3 billion per year due to IUU fishing.[8] Similar figures have also been published for Senegal,[9] Ghana[10] and Equatorial Guinea,[11] to name just three examples from West Africa.

It is beyond the scope of this book to provide more detailed insights into the problems related to research about IUU fishing. The examples outlined above nevertheless show the lack of reliable data, partly due to a limited amount of research that has been conducted on the subject for decades. At the same time, there can be no doubt that the economic impact of IUU fishing is significant, particularly in countries in sub-Saharan Africa where the overall GDP is relatively low, fish stocks are rich and governance of these natural resources is weak. In combination with opaque supply chains and a lack of oversight in ports where catches are later landed, including many ports in Europe, North America and Asia, IUU fishing offers high rewards, but much lower risks than other types of criminal activities at sea.

Social and Environmental Impacts

Figures and values quoted in the previous section may seem high, yet they 'understate the real social, economic and environmental costs of overfishing. Fisheries are crucial [...] in terms of livelihood and food security'.[12] Ghana's action plan against IUU fishing, published in 2014, illustrates that. The fisheries sector contributes at least 4.5% of the country's GDP and 'provides livelihood to an estimated 2.4 million people or 10% of the population'.[13] Most fisheries-related employment opportunities are linked to artisanal fishing,[14] underlining the direct link between healthy fish stocks and the income level of many families, particularly in coastal communities.

The situation may be even more critical in other countries throughout sub-Saharan Africa. The fishing sector is generally recognised as 'a critical source of employment, trade and food and nutrition security. In West Africa, up to a quarter of jobs are linked to fisheries',[15] and estimates for coastal countries in East Africa are similar. Clashes between artisanal fishermen and industrial fishing vessels are therefore commonplace, causing fishermen to lose their nets or even their boats when they are rammed by large trawlers.[16]

Firefights have also been reported, for example off Nigeria.[17] Such reports are almost impossible to verify, yet it is at least reasonable to assume that large fishing vessels are equipped with weapons for self-defence when they operate in an area where the threat of attacks against such vessels is significant. In Somalia, a deal between the government and the China Overseas Fisheries Association that was signed in December 2018 has even led to concerns about a return of piracy which might be justified as self-defence against industrial trawlers by local fishing communities.[18]

Environmental problems caused by IUU fishing are also severe. Highly destructive fishing techniques such as bottom-trawling or dredging are—unfortunately—highly effective, especially when bycatch is simply thrown overboard. Such practices often devastate marine habitats, yet crews involved in IUU fishing can simply move their vessels to other fishing grounds. Relevant authorities can only estimate the amounts of fish caught during such operations to determine sustainable catch levels for certain species, putting 'fisheries authorities at serious risk of over-licensing fishing access (…) and mismanaging the marine ecosystems'.[19]

In virtually all countries in East and West Africa, IUU fishing has 'wider impacts on food security, social welfare, fish stocks, marine environmental health, endangered species or the potential for political unrest in coastal communities'.[20] Economic diversification could mitigate some of these issues by providing other employment opportunities in fishing villages along the coastline of any given country. Small-scale projects, however, have not spread to create such opportunities. Moreover, 'discussions of diversifying coastal communities away from fishing seem to view fishing as just a livelihood and not a culture or a way of life'.[21] It is therefore important to combine the fight against IUU fishing with capacity-building efforts in the artisanal fishing sector. Such efforts could generate long-term gains for domestic populations, very likely outweighing the costs for better law enforcement in the EEZ. In short, investments into maritime security can create financial, environmental and social benefits.

4.1 Tackling the Problem

Rich fishing grounds can be found in the exclusive economic zones of many coastal states in East and West Africa. At the same time, navies and other maritime agencies generally have very few—if any—ships that are able to operate throughout the EEZ to monitor fishing activities, enforce the respective licences and detain vessels for severe infringements. Fisheries management is further complicated by a lack of clearly defined maritime boundaries, insufficient sharing of information and little harmonisation of regional frameworks which are necessary to ensure that fish stocks are not overexploited.[22]

Corruption is another factor that is often named by fishing experts. Corrupt officials can make it impossible to prosecute crews on vessels that were operating illegally, even when the necessary evidence is available. In other cases, fishing vessels are equipped with licences that were obtained with bribes, legalising operations that should otherwise be considered as IUU fishing. Finally, even without corruption there is often 'a lack of clarity over which agency has jurisdiction, and when vessels are caught enforcement is often not matched by judicial penalties'.[23]

Positive examples from both East and West Africa show that the fight against IUU fishing can indeed make progress. Providing better protection for vulnerable fish stocks and ensuring economic opportunities for artisanal fishermen as well as food security for the domestic population were some of the campaign promises made by Macky Sall before he was elected to his first term as Senegal's president in 2012. When his government came to power, the cancellation of 29 licences for foreign fishing vessels was one of the first administrative actions,[24] followed by efforts to improve governance of the fisheries sector to combat IUU fishing.[25]

In Ghana, the government was forced to act after the European Union—the largest export market for Ghana's fishing sector—issued a warning in 2013 that could have led to sanctions on fish caught or processed in Ghana.[26] After the Fisheries Enforcement Unit was formed in 2013,[27] a comprehensive plan was published in 2014 that includes various actions to combat IUU fishing.[28] Some issues remain, particularly a lack of transparency in the fisheries sector,[29] yet the fight against IUU fishing will also have a prominent role in the National Integrated Maritime Strategy that was under development at the time of writing. The strategy is supposed to include a broad range of actions against different types of criminal activities at sea, including most of the measures against IUU fishing that have already been defined in 2014.[30]

In East Africa, examples from Mozambique and Madagascar illustrate that problems with IUU fishing can be very different on the national level. Measures that may work in one country are therefore not necessarily effective elsewhere. IUU fishing in Mozambique is widespread among domestic fishermen. Most of their catch is intended for sale on local markets, giving authorities the opportunity to act. However, community fisheries councils play an important role for fisheries governance. These organisations have to balance their members' short-term concerns with the long-term sustainability of fish stocks.[31] The latter part is often complicated because many fishermen are already struggling to catch enough fish to survive and earn money for their families.[32]

On the other side of the Mozambique Channel, Madagascar faces very different challenges. IUU fishing in the country's EEZ, often conducted by foreign fishing vessels, puts pressure on the artisanal fishing sector.[33] Resources to protect fish stocks, however, are completely insufficient for an island nation that stretches about 1500 kilometres from north to south. In 2014, the Africa Progress Panel summarised that 'Madagascar's exclusive coastal zone (…) is overseen by 3 small monitoring vessels, 8 speedboats, 18 inspectors and 22 observers'[34] and the situation has not dramatically improved since then.

Together with six other coastal countries from the region, Mozambique and Madagascar are part of Fish-I Africa, an initiative supported by several non-governmental organisations with an environmental focus. Fish-I Africa was formed in 2012 as an informal and intergovernmental network to improve cooperation as well as the sharing of information and intelligence among relevant authorities in all participating countries. Several detailed investigations have underlined the problems with IUU fishing in the western Indian Ocean. At the same time, Fish-I Africa's work shows that it is possible to achieve at least some success when government agencies from different countries pool their limited resources to combat a problem that cuts across national—and maritime—boundaries.[35]

International Efforts and Partnerships

Efforts in East and West Africa are important to combat IUU fishing, but these will only be sustainable when they are complemented by international efforts. Some of these efforts are even a legal requirement. In April 2015, the International Tribunal for the Law of the Sea (ITLOS) underlined that any country has 'the obligation to take necessary measures (…) to ensure compliance by vessels flying its flag'[36] with regulations set up by coastal states or regional fisheries management organisations. Flag states are also obliged to investigate reports about specific vessels which are suspected to be involved in IUU fishing. Representatives from environmental organisations immediately recognised the importance of the ITLOS ruling, summarising it as 'a real game changer'.[37]

Six years earlier, an international convention had already been adopted by the United Nations' Food and Agriculture Organization (FAO). The Port States Measures Agreement (PSMA) has been described as a 'critical tool in the worldwide fight against illegal fishing',[38] yet it only entered into force in 2016 after it had been ratified by 25 countries.[39] One of the PSMA's main goals is to ensure that fishing vessels can only land their catch in designated ports. Ships that have been involved in IUU fishing are supposed to be completely blocked from accessing ports. Information is also supposed to be shared with authorities in other countries. Whether these intentions will become reality remains at least questionable. Many countries affected by IUU fishing suffer from a lack of financial and human resources, yet 'a treaty is only as good as the parties that ratify and enforce it'[40] and there is no guarantee that signatories will make additional resources available.

Some examples, however, give rise to optimism. In South Korea, a warning issued by the European Union in 2013 led to unprecedented measures, aimed at preventing vessels flying the South Korean flag or owned by domestic companies to be involved in IUU fishing. Among other things, all fishing vessels registered in the country are fitted with an electronic logbook. Information on fishing operations or catch data can therefore be shared in real time. Involvement in illegal fishing activities has also become a criminal offence. Rather than merely paying fines, masters and owners now face potential prison sentences of up to five years when they are convicted of involvement in such operations.[41]

The European Union has also introduced a new system to improve the visibility of fishing vessels which are registered in EU member states. Among other things, vessel owners have to obtain authorisation from their flag state before starting to fish in the EEZ of a third country or on the high seas where no national jurisdiction applies. The respective flag state has to consider several criteria, including a potential history of involvement in IUU fishing.[42] One of the key drivers of these new regulations was the ITLOS advisory opinion mentioned above.

Despite progress in some areas, much work remains to be done to enable coastal countries with limited resources to combat IUU fishing. Even without the necessary assets to patrol the EEZ, coastal states could at least track and monitor fishing operations with electronic means. Identification of fishing vessels, however, is often impossible because there is no global standard that requires owners to obtain a unique vessel identifier similar to the IMO number for merchant ships.[43] Other information to identify a ship, for example the name, the flag or the call sign, can easily be changed. In practice, that provides owners and masters with the opportunity to disguise the real identity of specific vessels.

In the meantime, some countries in sub-Saharan Africa have joined forces with environmental organisations to combat IUU fishing at sea. The governments of Gabon and Sao Tomé and Principe, for example, started a partnership with Sea Shepherd in 2016 that has resulted in annual operations. As part of Operation Albacore, Sea Shepherd provides a ship which is used as a platform for law enforcement personnel,[44] a model that has since been transferred to other countries. In Tanzania, Sea Shepherd even conducted patrols for six months in 2018, together with personnel from various security agencies and in cooperation with Fish-I Africa.[45] Such efforts have led to the organisation being labelled a 'non-state navy',[46] yet other environmental NGOs have been involved in similar projects.[47]

While such projects generate headlines in the media and attention from the general public, the long-term solution to IUU fishing can only be on land. Fishing vessels have to land their catch as their operations would not be commercially viable otherwise. Technical means to ensure a transparent supply chain are now widely available and easily affordable. Enforcing such transparency, however, is complicated, illustrated by the limited number of countries that have ratified the Port State Measures Agreement and the fact that it took seven years after the adoption for the agreement to finally come into force.

4.2 Summary

This chapter contains only a very brief summary of problems caused by IUU fishing. It is beyond the scope of this book to provide a deeper analysis of these issues, including the knock-on effects on land or potential links with other maritime challenges, namely piracy.[48] Nevertheless, some direct links between IUU fishing and a lack of maritime security are clearly visible. Sustainable solutions are unlikely to be found unless IUU fishing is addressed on the national, the regional and the international level in more or less equal measure.

In relation to maritime security, four aspects of IUU fishing deserve particular attention. First, there is a disconnect between naval operations, merchant shipping and fishing activities. Crews on merchant vessels frequently report certain incidents as suspicious, even though these are clearly linked to typical fishing patterns. In areas where the threat of attacks is relatively high, for example in the Gulf of Aden or off Nigeria, such reports may create a perception of an even higher threat level.[49] At the same time, navies engaged in counter-piracy operations often have to adhere to a strict mandate and are rarely interested in IUU fishing or other types of criminal activities at sea. In the past, the European Union's counter-piracy forces in the Indian Ocean did not even share data gathered during their operations with regional fisheries authorities or organisations such as Fish-I Africa.[50]

The second important aspect is the lack of reliable data related to fish stocks in general and IUU fishing in particular, particularly in countries throughout sub-Saharan Africa. Sustainable management of fish stocks requires scientific data, and catch levels for certain species are otherwise merely estimates. Subsidies in the fisheries sector add to the complexity, summarised by the former US ambassador to the World Trade Organization, Peter Allgeier: 'In areas such as agriculture or manufacturing, one country's subsidised production (…) gives the subsidising country's producers a competitive advantage. In the fishing sector, (…) such practices rob the other countries of production resources by depleting the fisheries that are everyone's resource base'.[51]

Another problem is the fact that IUU fishing is an almost victimless crime. Managing fish stocks means that relevant authorities have to deal with the 'tragedy of the commons'; crews on foreign fishing vessels in particular have no incentive to limit the exploitation of marine resources in a specific area. Owners of industrial fishing vessels profit from IUU fishing while the domestic population (and future generations) have to bear the costs. In countries throughout East and West Africa, they may even be emboldened 'by the inaction of states that are unwilling or unable to carry out their regulatory responsibilities'.[52] The situation is unlikely to change significantly until national governments begin to address IUU fishing as a transnational organised crime rather than a statutory offence, giving law enforcement agencies additional incentives to get involved. Currently, IUU fishing carries low risks for offenders, 'crime linked to the fisheries value chain will not be investigated because it is not seen as a major priority and it is difficult to investigate'.[53]

Finally, initiatives such as Fish-I Africa show that there is a need for improved regional cooperation of relevant authorities to combat IUU fishing, a problem that does not stop at the maritime boundary of any state. Enforcing domestic fisheries regulations is already a challenge in the artisanal sector. In Ghana, for example, an estimated 13,000 canoes are operated by small-scale fishermen.[54] Mozambique has about 600 landing sites stretched out along more than 2700 kilometres of coastline.[55] Relevant agencies therefore have to find additional resources to gather information about fish stocks, regulate industrial fishing activities and stop illegal practices, yet research and law enforcement at sea are the most expensive aspects in the management of fish stocks.

Technology could play an important role in the protection of fish stocks. In recent years, satellite surveillance has improved dramatically while costs have decreased significantly. Government agencies could use such data to target specific areas, limiting the need for patrols across the whole EEZ.[56] Information-sharing with regional partners is another example that does not even require the introduction of new technology.

Overall, governments do not have to spend vast amounts of money to combat IUU fishing. Small investments into better management and enhanced protection of fish stocks may be necessary, yet these are likely to pay dividends within a relatively short period of time. 'Restructuring fisheries management can increase economic output and efficiencies and improve livelihoods and food security by aligning the socio-economic incentives of fishermen and fishing communities with the biological health of fish stocks'[57]; in short: fish are a natural resource that provides food and jobs for the domestic population. Indonesia provides a very good example. After the government started a sustained campaign against IUU fishing in 2014, the domestic fisheries sector has grown faster than the overall GDP, fish consumption per capita has picked up and the average income of small-scale fishermen has increased.[58]

Governments unwilling to allocate more resources to the fight against IUU fishing are likely to face significant problems—and much higher costs—in the long term. Improving maritime security in general and tackling IUU fishing in particular requires a sustained effort. Benefits for domestic populations in coastal countries throughout East and West Africa are very likely to be much higher than the initial costs.

Notes

1. Examples include: de Coning, Eve, and Witbooi, Emma. 2015. "Towards a new 'fisheries crime' paradigm: South Africa as an illustrative example." *Marine Policy*, Vol. 60. 208–215; Haenlein, Cathy. *Below the surface: How illegal, unreported and unregulated fishing threatens our security.* London: RUSI, 2017; and Poling, Gregory, and Cronin, Conor. *Illegal, unreported and unregulated fishing as a national security threat.* Washington: CSIS, 2017.
2. Examples include: York, Geoffrey. 2015. Foreign trawlers encroaching on local fishing grounds off West African coast. *The Globe and Mail.* Available at: https://www.theglobeandmail.com/report-on-business/international-business/african-and-mideast-business/foreign-trawlers-enroaching-on-fishing-grounds-off-west-african-coast/article26766954/; Cosgrow, Wallace. 2015. FISH-I Africa is proving that coastal countries can halt large-scale illegal fishing. *The Huffington Post.* Available at: https://www.huffingtonpost.com/wallace-cosgrow/fish-i-africa-is-proving-that-coastal-countries_b_7472548.html; and Editorial Board. 2018. Illegal fishing is a global security threat. *Bloomberg.* Available at: https://www.bloomberg.com/opinion/articles/2018-12-28/illegal-fishing-is-a-global-security-threat.
3. Food and Agriculture Organization. *International plan of action to prevent, deter, and eliminate illegal, unreported and unregulated fishing (IPOA-IUU).* Rome: FAO/Fisheries and Aquaculture Department, 2001. 2–3.
4. Personal interview with expert on fisheries research, December 2018.
5. Personal interview with expert on fisheries research, December 2018.
6. Examples include: George, Rose. 2016. The marine, and human, costs of illegal fishing. *New Statesman.* Available at: https://www.newstatesman.com/culture/books/2016/02/marine-and-human-costs-illegal-fishing; World Wildlife Fund. *Living blue planet report: Species, habitats and human well-being.* Gland: WWF International, 2015.
7. Agnew, Pearce, Pramod et al. 2009. "Estimating the worldwide extent of illegal fishing." *PLoS ONE*, Vol. 4:2. 1–8.
8. Doumbouya, Camara, Mamie et al. 2017. "Assessing the effectiveness of monitoring control and surveillance of illegal fishing: The case of West Africa." *Frontiers in Marine Science*, Vol. 4:50. Available at: https://www.frontiersin.org/articles/10.3389/fmars.2017.00050/full.
9. Belhabib, Koutub, Sall et al. 2014. "Fisheries catch misreporting and its implications." *Fisheries Research*, Vol. 151. 1–11.
10. Nunoo, Asiedu, Amador et al. *Reconstruction of marine fisheries catches for Ghana, 1950–2010.* Working Paper #2014–13. Vancouver: University of British Columbia, 2014.

11. Belhabib, Hellebrandt da Silva, Allison et al. 2016. "Filling a blank on the map: 60 years of fisheries in Equatorial Guinea." *Fisheries Management and Ecology*, Vol. 23. 119–132.
12. Spooner, Samantha. 2015. Fishy business in West African waters—and the bad guys are not always the usual suspects. *Mail & Guardian Africa*. Available at: https://whalesandmarinefauna.wordpress.com/2015/05/29/fishy-business-in-west-african-waters-and-the-bad-guys-are-not-always-the-usual-suspects/.
13. Republic of Ghana. 2014. National plan of action to prevent, deter, and eliminate illegal, unreported and unregulated fishing. Available at: http://www.fao.org/fishery/docs/DOCUMENT/IPOAS/national/Ghana/NPOA_IUU.pdf
14. Nunoo, Asiedu, Amador et al. *Reconstruction of marine fisheries catches for Ghana, 1950–2010*. 6.
15. Africa Progress Panel. *Grain, fish, money—Financing Africa's green and blue revolutions*. Geneva: Africa Progress Panel, 2014. 89.
16. Kende-Robb, Caroline. 2014. Why illegal fishing off Africa's coast must be stopped. *The Guardian*. Available at: https://www.theguardian.com/global-development/poverty-matters/2014/jun/19/why-illegal-fishing-africa-must-be-stopped; Gulled, Yusuf Abdilahi. 2015. Illegal fishing in the shadow of piracy. *Centre for Security Studies*. Available at: https://isnblog.ethz.ch/business-and-finance/illegal-fishing-in-the-shadow-of-piracy.
17. Okhomina, Osa. 2016. Piracy-armed attacks from foreign fishing trawlers spark violent protests in Bayelsa. *Leadership*. Available at: https://allafrica.com/stories/201602030805.html.
18. Dahir, Abdi Latif. 2018. China will start fishing along Somalia's coastline just as piracy makes a comeback. *Quartz Africa*. Available at: https://qz.com/africa/1506419/somalia-gives-fishing-license-to-31-china-vessels/; Bagnetto, Laura Angela. 2019. Somalia: Chinese deal angers fishing communities, sparks concerns over sovereignty and piracy. *RFI*. Available at: http://en.rfi.fr/africa/20190207-Somalia-Chinese-deal-angers-fishing-communities-sparks-concerns-over-sovereignty-and.
19. Nunoo, Asiedu, Amador et al. *Reconstruction of marine fisheries catches for Ghana, 1950–2010*. 21.
20. Copeland, Douglas. 2014. "Accounting for net losses." *The World Today*, Vol. 70:1. 20.
21. Akyeampong, Emmanuel. "Indigenous knowledge and maritime fishing in West Africa: The case of Ghana." In: Boon, Emmanuel, and Hens, Luc (eds.). *Indigenous knowledge systems and sustainable development: Relevance for Africa*. Delhi: Kamla-Raj Enterprises, 2007. 173.
22. Personal interview with expert on fisheries research, December 2018.

23. Copeland, Douglas. "Accounting for net losses." 20.
24. Vidal, John. 2012. Senegal revokes licences of foreign fishing trawlers. *The Guardian*. Available at: https://www.theguardian.com/environment/2012/may/04/senegal-revokes-licences-foreign-fishing-vessels.
25. Seck, Madjiguene. 2016. Senegal takes steps to establish a sustainable and better-governed fisheries sector. *World Bank*. Available at: http://www.worldbank.org/en/news/feature/2016/08/08/senegal-takes-steps-to-establish-a-sustainable-and-better-governed-fisheries-sector.
26. No author. 2015. EU issues 'green card' to Ghana on fisheries management. *Stop Illegal Fishing*. Available at: https://stopillegalfishing.com/press-links/eu-issues-green-card-to-ghana-on-fisheries-management/.
27. Crabbe, Victor. 2013. Ministry of Fisheries inaugurates enforcement unit. *Modern Ghana*. Available at: https://stopillegalfishing.com/press-links/eu-issues-green-card-to-ghana-on-fisheries-management/.
28. Republic of Ghana. 2014. *National Plan of Action*.
29. Environmental Justice Foundation and Hen Mpoano. 2019. Securing equitable and sustainable fisheries. *Report under the Far Dwuma Nkodo (Securing Sustainable Fisheries) project*. Available at: https://ejfoundation.org//resources/downloads/EJF-Ghana-transparency-position-paper-HM-final.pdf.
30. Personal interview with representative from a Ghanaian NGO directly providing assistance to various government departments involved with the new strategy, November 2018. The author has also given presentations at workshops for government representatives, organized by the NGO.
31. For a comprehensive overview of the artisanal fishing sector in Mozambique, see Benkenstein, Alex. *Small-scale fisheries in a modernising economy: Opportunities and challenges in Mozambique*. Johannesburg: SAIIA, 2013.
32. No author. 2014. Mozambique's small-scale fishermen battle headwinds. *The New Humanitarian*. Available at: https://www.thenewhumanitarian.org/news/2014/01/22/mozambique-s-small-scale-fishermen-battle-headwinds.
33. Le Manach, Gough, Harris et al. 2012. "Unreported fishing, hungry people and political turmoil: The recipe for a food security crisis in Madagascar?" *Marine Policy*, Vol. 36:1. 218–219.
34. Africa Progress Panel. *Grain, Fish, Money*. 92.
35. The initiative wants continue its work in the coming years, mainly by supporting investigations and actions and by the provision of relevant analysis. For a more detailed overview, see Stop Illegal Fishing. *Fish-I Africa: Our future*. Gaborone: Stop Illegal Fishing, 2017.

36. International Tribunal for the Law of the Sea. *Case No. 21—Request for an advisory opinion submitted by the Sub-Regional Fisheries Commission (SRFC)*. Hamburg: ITLOS, 2015. 60.
37. Battle, Jessica. 2015. Tribunal throws lifeline to coastal states facing foreign vessel threats to fisheries. *WWF International*. Available at: http://wwf.panda.org/?243590/Tribunal-throws-lifeline-to-coastal-states-facing-foreign-vessel-threats-to-fisheries.
38. Lopez, Jaime. 2015. Costa Rice ratifies UN treaty to fight illegal fishing. *The Costa Rica Star*. Available at: https://news.co.cr/costa-rica-ratifies-un-treaty-to-fight-illegal-fishing/43318/.
39. United Nations. 2016. UN agency announced world's first illegal fishing treaty now in force. *UN News*. Available at: https://news.un.org/en/story/2016/06/531252-un-agency-announces-worlds-first-illegal-fishing-treaty-now-force#.WGGQHLF0cyk.
40. Vosburgh, Kimberly. 2014. Why—and how—to ratify the Port State Measures Agreement. *Pew Trusts*. Available at: https://www.pewtrusts.org/en/research-and-analysis/articles/2014/06/02/why-and-how-to-ratify-the-port-state-measures-agreement. A detailed list of countries that have already ratified the PSMA or that have initiated the ratification process can also be found on the Pew Trusts website at: https://www.pewtrusts.org/en/research-and-analysis/data-visualizations/2014/psma.
41. EJF Staff. Bold action taken by Korea to combat illegal, unreported and unregulated (IUU) fishing shows EU IUU regulation is working. *Environmental Justice Foundation*. Available at: https://ejfoundation.org/news-media/2015/bold-action-taken-by-korea-to-combat-illegal-unreported-and-unregulated-iuu-fishing-shows-eu-iuu-regulation-is-working.
42. No author. 2015. Commission proposes new rules to improve transparency and monitoring of EU fleet fishing internationally. *European Commission*. Available at: http://europa.eu/rapid/press-release_IP-15-6266_en.htm.
43. Some flag states require IMO numbers for fishing vessels, similar to merchant ships. Fishing licences in some regions also require an IMO number for every licensed vessel, and the IMO number scheme was extended in 2018 to cover additional fishing vessels, yet the application remains voluntary in many cases.
44. Sea Shepherd. 2019. About Operation Albacore III. Available at: https://www.seashepherdglobal.org/our-campaigns/operation-albacore/learn-more/.
45. No author. 2018. Sea Shepherd launches operation Jodari with Tanzania, makes first three arrests. *Stop Illegal Fishing*. Available at: https://stopillegalfishing.com/press-links/sea-shepherd-launches-operation-jodari-tanzania-makes-first-three-arrests/.

46. Rawley, Chris, and Berube, Claude. 2013. The non-state navy: Sea Shepherd as a case study for twenty-first-century maritime non-state actors. *Small Wars Journal*. Available at: https://smallwarsjournal.com/jrnl/art/the-non-state-navy-sea-shepherd-as-a-case-study-for-21st-century-maritime-non-state-actors.
47. Greenpeace Africa. 2017. Hope in West Africa ship tour briefer. Available at: https://www.greenpeace.org/africa/en/publications/1941/hope-in-west-africa-ship-tour-briefer/.
48. Denton, Ginger, and Harris, Jonathan. 2019. "The impact of illegal fishing on maritime piracy: Evidence from West Africa." *Studies in Conflict and Terrorism* (Published online).
49. Personal interview with maritime security analyst, January 2019.
50. Personal interview with representative from an environmental NGO involved in activities against IUU fishing, October 2017.
51. Allgeier, Peter. 2014. "Trade and environmental sustainability: The case for addressing fisheries subsidies." *Bridges Africa*, Vol. 3:4. 8–9.
52. Kende-Robb, Caroline. Why illegal fishing off Africa's coast must be stopped.
53. United Nations Office on Drugs and Crime. 2017. Stretching the fishnet: Identifying opportunities to address fisheries crime. *Conference edition*. Available at: https://fishcrime.com/wp-content/uploads/2017/07/Stretching-the-Fishnet.pdf. 28.
54. Gibbah, Godfred Blay. 2019. Resource FEU to deal with illegal fishing at sea—Tema chief fisherman. *Ghanaian Times*. Available at: https://allafrica.com/stories/201901150710.html.
55. Benkenstein, Alex. *Small-scale fisheries in a modernising economy*. 8.
56. Gunawardene, Nalaka. 2016. Technology can help resolve South Asia's fishing wars. *SciDevNet*. Available at: https://www.scidev.net/south-asia/fisheries/columns/technology-can-help-resolve-south-asia-s-fishing-wars.html.
57. Global Environment Facility. 2014. Report on the sixth replenishment of the GEF Trust Fund. *Fifth GEF Assembly*, 28–29 May 2014. Available at: https://www.thegef.org/sites/default/files/council-meeting-documents/GEF.A.5.07.Rev_.01_Report_on_the_Sixth_Replenishment_of_the_GEF_Trust_Fund_May_22_2014_1.pdf. 131.
58. Santosa, Achmad. 2018. Combating IUU fishing and fisheries crime. *Presentation at the 4th international symposium on fisheries crime*. Available at: https://fishcrime.com/wp-content/uploads/2018/11/Combating-IUU-Fishing-Fisheries-Crime.pdf.

CHAPTER 5

Growing Together

Abstract This chapter concentrates on the current state of maritime security in East and West Africa. Several examples for efforts to improve security at sea through better cooperation on the regional level are provided, highlighting the shortcomings that have to be addressed in the coming years. It also stresses the lack of available data about even the most basic issues which further complicates the response to security challenges at sea. Cooperation efforts across both regions covered in this book are also outlined. These are often not directly concerned with maritime security issues, yet provide a broader context of regional integration in both East and West Africa. Documents like the *Djibouti Code of Conduct* or the *Yaoundé Code of Conduct* can only be implemented in frameworks provided by existing organisations, particularly the Regional Economic Communities endorsed by the African Union. Moreover, the involvement and interests of actors from outside East or West Africa have to be considered for a realistic analysis.

Keywords Regional integration · Regional economic communities · *Djibouti Code of Conduct* · *Yaoundé Code of Conduct*

This chapter looks at the current state of maritime security and efforts to improve regional cooperation in East and West Africa. As mentioned throughout the previous chapters, it underlines that maritime security has started to attract increasing interest from academics and practitioners

D. Siebels, *Maritime Security in East and West Africa*,
https://doi.org/10.1007/978-3-030-22688-6_5

over the past decade after it had been largely ignored previously. Moreover, this chapter highlights again that it is complicated—and sometimes impossible—to find reliable data even about seemingly basic issues, for example the actual number of attacks against merchant ships or the estimated extent of Illegal, Unreported and Unregulated (IUU) fishing in any country's Exclusive Economic Zones (EEZ).

Despite such shortcomings, there is no question that most issues related to maritime security vary significantly on the national level.[1] As a consequence, it is impossible to define a standard of maritime security which can be used as a measure for all countries in East and West Africa. Improved coordination with other regional countries or, in some cases, with international partners can nevertheless be a boost for national capabilities. Cooperation efforts across both regions covered in this book are outlined in the subsequent sections and placed into a broader context that is not directly concerned with, but relevant for maritime security issues.

Large parts of the content in this chapter can be found in open sources, including policy papers, official treaties, academic papers or media reports. Gathering such information, however, is often complicated for any research topics covering sub-Saharan Africa. Websites of regional economic communities or even the African Union offer much less content than online portals run by organisations such as the European Union; the same is true on the level of national governments or government agencies.

Furthermore, any open-source information needs to be put in context and should be compared with the situation 'on the ground' as often as possible. Ratifying a multilateral treaty is not the same as implementing it. Statements by international organisations are often driven by political ambitions rather than realistic assessments. Political discussions may have a domestic context that outsiders fail to appreciate. This chapter therefore relies on background knowledge gathered during seminars, conferences and most notably interviews conducted over several years, leading to a multifaceted view of maritime security in East and West Africa.

5.1 New Topic of Interest

Pirate attacks off African coastlines have been extensively covered by media reports for more than a decade. In 2009, *Time* magazine explained 'How Somalia's fishermen became pirates'.[2] Five years later,

The Economist analysed 'The ungoverned seas' around Africa,[3] *Al Jazeera* then published a documentary on 'Piracy in Nigeria' in 2016.[4]

Many more examples can be found by a quick online search, generally showing that pirate attacks against merchant ships started to generate widespread interest due to the actions of Somalia-based groups from 2007 onwards. When the number of attacks off Somalia started to decrease significantly from 2012 onwards, the attention shifted to West Africa where the majority of violent attacks against merchant ships have taken place more recently. Most media reports, however, fail to mention that such incidents have been a problem in the region for decades. The International Maritime Organization's first resolution about piracy and armed robbery at sea—adopted in the early 1980s—was mainly concerned with attacks against merchant vessels operating in West Africa.[5]

Media reports also played an important role for increased political interest. In February 2019, that even led to the first-ever UN Security Council debate about the 'global challenge of transnational maritime crime'.[6] While it did not lead to concrete outcomes, the debate once again emphasised that pirate attacks are merely one indicator for a lack of maritime security rather than a key symptom, even though such attacks generate far more attention than issues like smuggling or IUU fishing.

Governments in East and West Africa have at least started to address the shortage of naval assets, human resources and the necessary equipment for day-to-day operations in recent years. Awareness of issues related to maritime security has increased, albeit the reasons are different on the national level. In countries like Ghana[7] or Mozambique,[8] offshore oil and gas discoveries led to increased attention on maritime matters. In Benin[9] or Togo,[10] investments into port infrastructure and the importance of international trade links provided good reasons for governments to focus on related issues. Protection of fish stocks is key for governments in Senegal[11] or the Seychelles.[12]

None of these countries faces only one issue caused by a lack of security at sea. In most cases, however, it is possible to identify one area where impacts are particularly severe which in turn creates an incentive for governments to become more involved. Even with additional resources, it is very likely to take several years to increase national capabilities and improve regional integration to a level that enables governments to comprehensively address maritime security issues. For the time being, discussions about security remain focused on land-based issues, and navies therefore remain the 'poor little brothers' of armies, highlighted by the relatively low number of naval personnel in the armed forces of most countries in East and West Africa.

Table 5.1 merely shows personnel strength which is not a perfect measure. The navy's budget share of the overall defence budget may be higher, and other services sometimes have responsibility for maritime matters; for example, surveillance at sea is sometimes conducted by the air force. The overall organisation of the armed forces and civilian agencies such as coastguards or the *gendarmerie navale* (in francophone countries) should also be noted.

As a general indicator for long-term political priorities, however, the table is very useful. Despite an increasing focus on the blue economy and its contribution to economic growth and development, the navy's share of overall military personnel is rarely above 10%; in most countries, it is significantly lower. In short, armies are more significant for governments, often due to large-scale military involvement in the provision of domestic security rather than the defence against external threats.[13]

Table 5.1 Naval personnel in relation to armed forces personnel

Country	*Personnel armed forces*	*Naval personnel*	*Naval personnel (percentage of armed forces overall)*
West Africa (selected countries)			
Angola	107,000	1000	0.9
Benin	7250	500	6.9
Cameroon	15,400	1500	9.7
Côte d'Ivoire	27,400	1000	3.6
DR Congo	134,250	6700	5
Ghana	15,500	2000	12.9
Nigeria	135,000	25,000	18.5
Senegal	13,600	950	7
Sierra Leone	8500	200 (maritime wing)	2.4
Togo	8550	200	2.3
East Africa (selected countries)			
Djibouti	10,450	200	1.9
Kenya	24,100	1600	6.6
Madagascar	13,500	500	3.7
Mozambique	11,200	200	1.8
Tanzania	27,000	1000	3.7

International Institute for Strategic Studies. *The Military Balance. Chapter Nine: Sub-Saharan Africa*. London: IISS, 2019. 438–502. https://data.worldbank.org/indicator/NY.GDP.PETR.RT.ZS?end=2016&start=2012&year_low_desc=true

Questionable Donations, Problematic Statistics

Operational and tactical shortcomings may be relatively easy to address. At the same time, navies and coastguards throughout East and West Africa often have to operate equipment that was provided as hand-me-downs from Western navies. Two former US Coast Guard cutters which were given to the Nigerian Navy in 2012 and 2014, respectively,[14] as part of the *Excess Defence Articles Program* are perfect examples. These ships were hailed by US officials to 'have bolstered maritime security in Nigeria',[15] yet both vessels had originally been commissioned in 1968 and require extremely high expenses for day-to-day operations and maintenance. On its official website, the US Coast Guard even states that it has 'avoided more than $120 million in disposal costs'[16] for decommissioned ships between 1997 and 2018. These vessels were handed over to various partner nations, including many African countries.

Aside from high operating costs, donated naval vessels can lead to another problem. When these ships were originally commissioned, weapons systems and operational capabilities were designed based on specific requirements, demanding the availability of trained personnel and regular exercises. For recipients of donated warships, however, these conditions may be too demanding or simply irrelevant. Moreover, naval vessels are usually part of complicated logistics chains, and spare parts may not be readily available when merely the platform is handed over to a new owner. In short, donated ships are not a good solution to address maritime security requirements in East and West Africa, leading to a hotchpotch of ship types rather than naval fleets that were carefully assembled based on strategic requirements and available resources for recurring costs.

Regarding actual security requirements, piracy and armed robbery at sea are a highly visible illustration for a lack of security at sea, even though attacks against merchant ships are not the most pressing maritime security concern for African governments. Reliable information about the actual number of attacks, however, is not easy to find. An analysis of current threat levels or historic trends is therefore very complicated, illustrated by the situation in West Africa.

Different organisations provide statistics about piracy and armed robbery at sea across the region. Notable examples include:

- The International Maritime Bureau's Piracy Reporting Centre (IMB PRC), a non-profit organisation, largely funded by donations from the maritime industry.
- Maritime Domain Awareness for Trade—Gulf of Guinea (MDAT-GoG), a reporting centre which is manned by naval personnel from the UK and France.
- Risk Intelligence, a leading security intelligence company which provides information about specific incidents, threat assessments and related reports through the Risk Intelligence System, a subscription-based online portal mainly used by shipping and insurance companies as well as government agencies.[17]

All of these organisations utilise different sources and have different requirements for attacks to be included in their respective statistics. Moreover, the same incident may be categorised in different ways, making it impossible to compare different sets of statistics as shown in Fig. 5.1.

Figures collected by the IMB PRC, for example, are often quoted in media reports and even academic articles,[18] mainly because they are available for free. These figures, however, do not completely reflect the situation. In 2015, the IMB PRC's Director Pottengal Mukundan

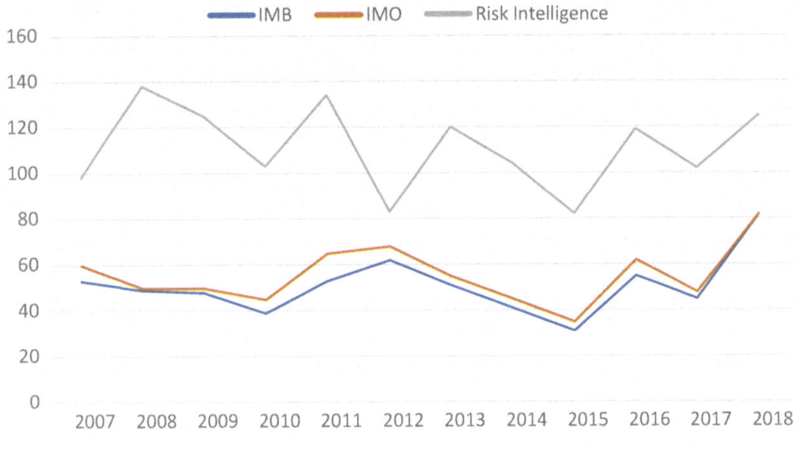

Fig. 5.1 Maritime security incidents in West Africa (Senegal to Angola) recorded by different organisations, 2007–2018 (*Source* Compiled by author)

assumed that around 70% of all incidents in West Africa are not reported to the organisation.[19] At the same time, wide circulation of these statistics creates public and political attention for an issue that affects many shipping companies and seafarers on a daily basis.

Shipping companies often have good reasons for their reluctance to submit reports about attacks against their ships. Such incidents may lead to reputational damage and can therefore have commercial implications. Another reason is a lack of trust in law enforcement agencies across West Africa, summarised by a former captain with many years of experience in the region: 'When we report a theft, we may have different agencies on our ship and are not even allowed to leave the port for a day or two. After a more serious incident, it is even worse and the last thing the captain wants is police or military on the ship. The crew has already been through a lot and investigations here [in West Africa] are not really subtle'.[20]

Political Shortcomings

It is certainly important to address shortcomings on the tactical and operational level to improve maritime security. Efforts on the political level, however, should not be disregarded either. Naval and law enforcement personnel have to act within a legal framework during operations and require the necessary funding from national governments. Laws to prosecute piracy cases are often mentioned in this context, especially after international actors convinced regional countries in East Africa to conduct trials against suspects who had been arrested by international naval forces trying to counter the threat of Somalia-based piracy.

Convictions during piracy trials have been described as an essential deterrent.[21] However, financial and technical assistance from international partners were the main reasons for countries like Kenya or the Seychelles to conduct trials involving Somali suspects. At the very least, it is debatable whether the prosecution of such complicated cases should have been handed over to countries where the justice system was already suffering from a lack of resources.[22]

Efforts to adjust or to introduce laws related to piracy cases have also been made in West Africa, again based on funding from international partners.[23] It should be noted that such laws are only relevant in genuine piracy cases, not for attacks against merchant ships inside territorial waters where many of these incidents take place. Even attacks on the high seas often involve other serious crimes that could also be prosecuted if suspects were later arrested. Finally, law enforcement capabilities of navies in West Africa are weak outside of territorial waters, creating challenges for prosecutors in an already overstretched justice system, even when relevant laws specifically covering piracy are in place.[24]

On a more general level, the lack of piracy-related laws is merely one symptom of a much broader issue. Any type of legislation in the maritime environment requires expertise and political will, yet governments throughout sub-Saharan Africa traditionally had very few incentives to get involved in maritime matters, explained in detail in the previous chapters. Historic limitations have made it even harder for governments to solve problems in the maritime environment which are transnational by nature. Ties with and political influence from former colonial powers have complicated regional cooperation for decades.[25]

An increasing awareness of maritime issues, also pointed out in the previous chapters, means that the situation has changed in recent years. Many countries have begun to improve governance of their respective maritime domains, for example by strengthening existing capabilities in civilian maritime organisations[26] or by improving law enforcement at sea through the provision of additional resources to navies and coastguards.[27]

Common interests and values are necessary to further improve cross-border cooperation on maritime issues, particularly in the sensitive area of security. Various problems, including the impacts of IUU fishing or the threat of attacks against merchant ships, have forced national governments to take a more proactive stance. Two codes of conduct which are supposed to enhance regional cooperation in both East and West Africa illustrate that shared interests in the maritime environment have been increasingly recognised in recent years.

5.2 Codes of Conduct for East and West Africa

Situation in East Africa

Piracy off Somalia started to be perceived as a problem by the international community around 2008. No less than four resolutions (1816, 1838, 1846 and 1851) were passed by the UN Security Council that year, encouraging various governments to become involved in naval operations to counter the threat. Within just a few months, warships from EU member states as well as from the United States, Japan, Russia, China, India and some other countries were active in the western part of the Indian Ocean.

At the same time, officials recognised that additional efforts were needed to tackle root causes of piracy on land. Throughout the region, there had already been some discussions about criminal activities at sea, involving an increasing number of governments from 2005 onwards. Three meetings had brought together participants from East Africa and the Arabian peninsula, assisted by the International Maritime Organization (IMO). Discussions involved a broad range of subjects, for example smuggling routes and IUU fishing, yet attacks off Somalia overshadowed these talks and 'the region chose to concentrate its efforts solely on the repression of piracy'.[28]

Representatives from nine countries in East Africa signed the *Djibouti Code of Conduct* (DCoC)[29] in January 2009, and eleven other countries from the western Indian Ocean region became signatories later. The IMO had originally pushed for a comprehensive document to address a broad range of maritime security issues, but governments in East Africa found it much easier to find common ground with a narrow focus on piracy as a common threat. Adopting the DCoC also created a chance to call for financial and technical assistance from international partners.[30]

Most of these partners knew from the outset that the DCoC signatories lacked the capacities to implement the provisions in the code. International donors therefore had to fund initiatives to create regional centres for information-sharing or to strengthen maritime law enforcement. At the same time, regional governments were not incentivised to prioritise maritime issues, leaving the sustainability of new initiatives in doubt. Donors—including many European countries, but also the United States or Japan—were nevertheless willing to provide funding to conduct piracy trials in the region[31] or to increase their military presence in a strategically important region.[32]

Situation in West Africa

Piracy and armed robbery at sea have been long-standing problems for merchant ships operating in West Africa. Governments across the region have also been concerned by other issues, first and foremost by IUU fishing and—in oil-producing countries—by security for offshore installations. Based on the experiences gathered in East Africa, government representatives therefore started to engage in discussions about a similar document for the region. Assistance from the IMO was important to bring members of two regional economic communities together: Economic Community of West African States (ECOWAS) in West Africa and Economic Community of Central African States (ECCAS) in Central Africa.

Negotiations took several years, but led to a document that was much more comprehensive than the DCoC. The code was formally adopted in June 2013 by 22 countries during a summit in Cameroon's capital Yaoundé; the city's name has since been used as shorthand for the cumbersome official title (*Code of Conduct concerning the repression of piracy, armed robbery against ships, and illicit maritime activity in West and Central Africa*). From the outset, the broad range of maritime security issues included in the *Yaoundé Code of Conduct* (YCoC) highlighted a need for cooperation between different agencies, both on the regional and on the national level.[33]

Even before the code was officially adopted, it was obvious that the signatories did not have the resources and capabilities to implement the necessary measures immediately. Governments nevertheless underlined their concerns about 'transnational organised crime in the maritime domain'[34] and—perhaps more importantly—recognised the international character of most criminal activities at sea.

Finally, the signatories had already been part of established regional blocs. Both ECOWAS and ECCAS suffer from a lack of resources and expertise, leading to a challenging environment for regional integration in very different political areas. These organisations, however, were at least useful to provide a framework for efforts to strengthen cooperation. For example, three maritime security zones and a regional coordination centre are supposed to be established in the ECOWAS region, modelled on a structure that was introduced by ECCAS already in 2009.[35]

Comparison

Comparing both codes described above highlights significant differences in purpose and scope, but also on the practical level. The YCoC was specifically designed to avoid any infringements on the sovereignty of signatories who 'should carry out their obligations (…) in a manner consistent with the principles of sovereign equality and territorial integrity'.[36] Similar specifications are not included in the DCoC, underlining that the document was almost exclusively aimed at piracy on the high seas and that assistance from outside actors was required from the outset.

In West Africa, measures on the national level are relatively well defined. Signatories pledged to implement national maritime policies, enabling them to fulfil the demands contained in two UN Security Council resolutions (2018 and 2039), adopted in 2011 and 2012, respectively. These resolutions had requested governments in the region to develop a comprehensive strategy to combat piracy and armed robbery at sea.

On the national level, many YCoC signatories did not have legislation in place to arrest suspects and put them on trial for piracy-related offences.[37] It has often been mentioned that criminals were therefore able to exploit legal loopholes and profit from a lack of regional cooperation.[38] On the practical level, however, efforts to introduce relevant laws were by and large a waste of resources. Prosecutions could generally be carried out on the basis of other laws, meaning that suspects may not be convicted for piracy and instead for kidnapping, armed robbery or other related offences. At the same time, any piracy-related court case is hampered by a lack of capacities in domestic judicial systems, law enforcement agencies and—more often than not—limited willingness of shipping companies, charterers and other commercial entities to fully cooperate with investigators and to provide transparent information about their own operations.[39]

Some other important aspects are also included in the YCoC. Measures related to the seizure of assets linked to illicit maritime activities or to limit opportunities for IUU fishing were completely missing from the DCoC when it was adopted in 2009. Signatories to the YCoC even included issues such as pollution prevention which is not a question of maritime security, yet very closely linked to capacities that will be most likely provided by national navies. It took signatories to the DCoC eight years before similar measures were finally adopted at a meeting in Jeddah in January 2017.[40]

One aspect that was not changed in 2017 was the use of the word 'participants' in the DCoC, compared to 'signatories' in the YCoC. Rather than a mere semantic issue, these words highlight a significant contrast. When the DCoC was adopted in 2009, centres such as *United Kingdom Maritime Trade Operations* (UKMTO), run by the Royal Navy, or the *Maritime Security Centre—Horn of Africa* (MSCHOA), run by the European Union, were already in place and played a vital role in the implementation of the code. In West Africa, no comparable infrastructure was available. Many signatories to the YCoC did not even have a designated focal point on the national level, complicating the response to alerts or requests. Governments in West Africa therefore recognised the need to enhance or introduce the necessary infrastructure.

Another important difference between both codes of conduct is the fact that existing regional institutions, namely ECOWAS and ECCAS, were taken into account. Neither of these organisations had much expertise in terms of maritime security, yet cooperation procedures on various topics had already been established, including on land-based security issues. In East Africa, the combination of coastal states, island nations and additional partners from the Arabian peninsula meant that cooperation efforts could not simply be built upon existing regional frameworks. In combination with the very narrow focus on counter-piracy operations that was the basis for cooperation until 2017, very few efforts to improve maritime security overall have been made within the region. Governments were happy to accept contributions from international partners, but it is at least questionable whether initiatives such as information-sharing centres will be sustainable in the long term without funding from outside partners.

5.3 Broader Context for Regional Approaches

The differences in both codes of conduct for East and West Africa provide insights into broader issues which have an impact on maritime security. Throughout both regions, governments have very different interests, yet they need to cooperate to improve security at sea. At the same time, maritime issues are generally not very important in the domestic context. Problems related to maritime security are therefore only prioritised when specific issues arise that need to be addressed immediately or when the blue economy offers additional—and obvious—revenues, notably when offshore oil or gas deposits are discovered.

Cooperation in the security sector is a contentious topic for governments around the world. Even within the European Union, where countries have decades of experience with economic cooperation and integration, decisions about the development of capabilities in the security sector are 'almost entirely national'.[41] Security cooperation is further complicated by the different nature of military resources—largely designed to be kept in a state of preparation—and civilian resources which are supposed to be in constant use.

At the heart of the problem is the Euro-centric concept of the nation state, largely developed between the seventeenth and nineteenth century. The provision of security for the domestic population is regarded as key for a functioning state. National governments are therefore often hesitant to agree on measures which could infringe their sovereign rights and, by extension, question their very existence. On the African continent, national sovereignty became an important issue when many former colonies gained independence in the 1950s and 1960s. Most of these countries 'were tied so closely to the financial or commercial leading strings of their former rulers as to enjoy little but the appearance of sovereignty',[42] further increasing the importance of seemingly independent decisions in the security sector.

In 2002, the African Union (AU) was created in its current format, replacing the Organization of African Unity. One of the AU's main objectives was the promotion of 'unity, solidarity, cohesion and cooperation among the peoples of Africa and African States'.[43] Due to the organisation's extremely diverse membership, regional economic communities (RECs) such as ECOWAS in West Africa or Intergovernmental Authority on Development (IGAD) in East Africa are supposed to be important building blocks of any continental initiative. By and large, these are not just smaller entities, but also have a less diverse membership with more common interests. Despite the label, RECs are not limited to economic questions. Cooperation within the security sector is another important area, underlined by regional training institutions, joint centres and even—in some cases—common peacekeeping missions.[44]

Any form of cooperation has to take the unique characteristics of sub-Saharan Africa into account. Most borders were randomly drawn by colonial powers, creating difficulties for many governments to uphold their domestic security monopoly and leading to bilateral conflicts. Examples include disputes between Cameroon and Nigeria over the Bakassi peninsula,[45] between Gabon and Equatorial Guinea over the Mbanié, Cocotiers and Congas islands,[46] or between Somalia and Ethiopia over the Ogaden region.[47]

Threats to sovereignty, both from within and outside, make it complicated for governments to transfer security-related tasks to regional or continental organisations. Improving cooperation therefore has to be based on tentative steps which often seem overly cautious to outsiders.

Progress is nevertheless possible, underlined by the DCoC and particularly the YCoC which has been commended by the AU's Peace and Security Council.[48]

On the operational level, cross-border cooperation between security agencies is equally complex. Organisational structures are often different, for example in anglophone and francophone countries.[49] Operations against IUU fishing vessels, for example, may be a responsibility of the navy or fall under the jurisdiction of a fisheries enforcement unit which is part of the ministry for agriculture. An overall lack of resources exacerbates these problems, but government representatives often want to avoid the embarrassment of admitting such issues.[50]

Regional Institutions in West Africa

Discussions over maritime security in West Africa which finally led to the YCoC involved ECOWAS and ECCAS as well as the Gulf of Guinea Commission (GGC) and the Maritime Organization for West and Central Africa (MOWCA). Except for ECOWAS and ECCAS, membership between these organisations overlaps, and based on their extremely limited organisational capacities, neither MOWCA nor the GGC should be expected to become a driving force behind improvements in maritime security across the region. The AU-recognised RECs—including their individual member states—will therefore have to shoulder much of the burden.

In the past decades, ECOWAS has arguably been the most visible African REC. Its founding treaty, revised in 1993, points out that the organisation's goals include better integration 'in all fields of socioeconomic activity (…), monetary, financial and fiscal policies' and 'the maintenance of peace, stability and security within the region'.[51] Security cooperation within ECOWAS dates back to the 1990s when the anglophone members contributed to an intervention force to end Liberia's civil war.[52] It is also one of five African RECs responsible for an own contingent that is part of the African Standby Force.[53]

In Central Africa, the equivalent REC is ECCAS, established in 1983 to 'promote and strengthen harmonious cooperation and balanced and self-sustained development in all fields of economic and social activity'.[54] Despite a similar mandate, organisational capacities are much lower than within ECOWAS.[55] Maritime security, however, has been an issue for member states since 2009 when a growing number of incidents led to a surveillance plan (SECMAR 1). Joint patrols and a regional cooperation centre in Pointe-Noire were initiated based on the plan which was followed by SECMAR 2 in 2011.[56]

Four ECCAS members (Cameroon, Equatorial Guinea, Gabon and Sao Tomé and Principe) which were most affected by criminal acts at sea were the main drivers of these discussions. All four countries contribute naval assets and personnel to a centre in Douala where joint efforts are coordinated. Operations against smuggling or IUU fishing are even conducted within territorial waters, despite bilateral disputes over maritime boundaries between Gabon and Equatorial Guinea as well as Equatorial Guinea and Cameroon.[57]

Positive results have been noted early on,[58] yet the fact that only one ship is supposed to be operational at any given time highlights the severe lack of resources. Financial restrictions and a lack of military assets, however, are not limited to the maritime environment.[59] ECCAS member states involved in the MICOPAX mission in the Central African Republic, conducted between 2008 and 2013, even had to rely on financial support from the European Union. It is therefore not reasonable to assume that significant improvements of maritime security can be achieved in the short term.

Regional Institutions in East Africa

Over the past decade, maritime matters have been even less of a topic for political debates in the region than in West Africa. With the exception of Mozambique and Tanzania, no country currently has the potential to develop a sizable offshore oil and gas industry. The number of large ports along the East African coastline is low, and fish stocks have by and large not been regarded as important ingredients for economic development over the past decades.

In 2010, the so-called Kampala Process was started, aimed at developing a comprehensive maritime strategy for Somalia which could have set an example for the region.[60] However, it was quickly brought to a standstill by a lack of cooperation between the federal government and regional administrations, particularly in Puntland and Somaliland. Both regions are seeking autonomy or even independence from the government in Mogadishu. The *United Nations Office on Drugs and Crime* (UNODC) then took over the secretariat function, and the entire process was rebranded as Regional Maritime Coordination Mechanism,[61] highlighting that it was largely driven by outside actors.

Other countries in the region have not prioritised maritime issues—or maritime security in particular—either. An institutional framework similar to West Africa has therefore not been created so far. Regional centres such as the *Regional Maritime Information Fusion Centre* (RMIFC) in Madagascar are mainly funded by external partners, largely based on the goal to suppress piracy in the western Indian Ocean. Existing RECs have rarely been part of the discussion so far.

There are two AU-recognised RECs in East Africa: The IGAD and the East African Community (EAC). IGAD's predecessor was founded in 1986 by six countries around the Horn of Africa. Eritrea and South Sudan joined the organisation in 1993 and 2011, respectively. Regional integration has never been high on IGAD's agenda, neither in economic terms nor in the security sector.[62] Security-related topics have become increasingly important in recent years, yet ambitions are often based on opportunities to attract funding from external partners.[63] 'The political will among member states to engage in real collaboration through IGAD is questionable'[64]; serious doubts about the long-term sustainability of any new initiatives are certainly justified.

Another problem for any type of integration within IGAD is the overlapping membership with the EAC through Kenya and Uganda. Together with Tanzania, both countries revived the organisation in 2000 after it had collapsed more than two decades earlier. In 2007, Rwanda and Burundi also joined the EAC. In terms of economic integration, the organisation has achieved remarkable success.[65] Security cooperation has also been a topic, leading to joint military exercises and joint border patrols on land.[66] However, various divisions within the EAC 'are likely to paralyze the ability (…) to act decisively on issues related to peace and security'.[67] Maritime security is also likely to remain a niche topic because three of the five members are landlocked countries.

The threat of Somalia-based piracy raised governments' attention across the region, often because foreign donors were seeking for regional partners to implement counter-piracy programmes. The Contact Group on Piracy off the Coast of Somalia (CGPCS) provides a good example. The CGPCS was established as a forum for national governments, international organisations and the shipping industry, aimed at coordinating political and military efforts to combat piracy in the western Indian Ocean. It has been described as 'a transient, issue-focused, political-level voluntary coordination body'[68] with a limited focus.

Participants in the CGPCS, however, were mainly actors from outside the region with an interest in counter-piracy efforts. Discussions were therefore mainly centred on issues as they were recognised by international partners rather than regional governments,[69] exemplified by a report about lessons over the previous years, published in 2014.[70] Out of ten articles, only one contains a regional—in this case Somali—perspective,[71] a token effort to create a sense of regional ownership.

For some countries in the region, involvement in the fight against piracy quickly became a worthwhile effort. The government of the Seychelles in particular was keen to accept foreign assistance, often linked to the prosecution of suspected pirates. The Regional Anti-Piracy Prosecutions and Intelligence Coordination Centre (RAPPICC) was launched in early 2012, funded with a US$1 million grant that was provided by the UK government.

RAPPICC's role was later extended to cover other types of criminal activities at sea, reflected in a name change to Regional Fusion and Law Enforcement Centre for Safety and Security at Sea (REFLECS3). Aside from the direct funding of the centre, it was also an important exhibit for international cooperation when the EU provided a US$6.4 million grant for sustainable development in the Seychelles.[72] Activities at REFLECS3, however, have been very limited so far, and the centre is little more than a flagship project for foreign donors.

The Djibouti Regional Training Centre (DRTC) is a similar example. It was supposed to be a centre for joint training exercises and regional workshops, yet it was only opened in 2015 after four years of planning and construction. Activities are by and large limited to seminars and conferences sponsored by international partners rather than regional partners or the government of Djibouti. In November 2017, it was even reported that an IMO official had warned 'that the DRTC is increasingly viewed as a failed project'.[73]

Looking at the DRTC's genesis, it is not surprising that the centre failed to attract more interest from the region. Funding for the project was provided by the IMO's Djibouti Code of Conduct Trust Fund which in turn was largely financed by donations from Japan's government. These donations were already promised ahead of the DCoC's adoption in 2009 and implicitly linked to the construction of relevant infrastructure in Djibouti where a Japanese naval base was opened in 2011 and expanded in 2015. An additional expansion was then announced in 2018.[74] Requirements of regional navies were not taken into consideration when the centre's location was determined. For Japan's government, funding for the DRTC was merely a vehicle to gain access to a strategically important region. Officials in Djibouti were happy to accept the money for the construction, even though their interest in using the facilities remains limited at best.

Finally, the introduction of various centres for information-sharing was also part of the DCoC's implementation phase. Several centres were supported by donors, yet the initial plan with three centres based in Yemen, Kenya and Tanzania and the assignment of specific countries to these centres did not take existing RECs into account. In Somalia, a split between Somaliland and Puntland reporting to the centre in Yemen and the southern part of the country being assigned to the centre in Kenya even threatened to increase tensions between the federal and regional governments.[75]

Plans for several centres to coordinate and share information were never fully implemented. These functions have since been taken over by the Regional Maritime Information Fusion Centre (RMIFC), largely funded through the European Union's €37 million MASE programme.[76] Madagascar was chosen as host country for the RMIFC in 2015 after a diplomatic battle with the Seychelles where the government agreed to host the Regional Centre for Co-ordination (RCOC) instead.[77] Funding for the RCOC was also provided through the MASE programme, yet interest from the region to use this centre without a clearly defined role has so far been limited at best.[78]

Overall, the involvement of and funding from international partners, particularly the European Union, has been key for the establishment of regional centres as well as for related programmes, for example the IORIS software. The system was developed as a platform for shared information and secure communications, funded through the EU's CRIMARIO project. The European Union agreed to pay for running costs until March 2020,[79] but at the time of writing, there was no commitment from regional partners to provide the necessary budget for continued use. Similar software tools had already been used by most navies in the region before IORIS was officially launched in 2018, and other forms of communication—including personal interactions via popular messaging apps such as WhatsApp or Telegram—are often used for coordination purposes in practice. These methods may be imperfect solutions, yet they are much more suited to the needs of navies and other maritime agencies with very limited budgets and available assets.[80] Furthermore, despite increasing recognition for maritime topics, there is still a lack of political will to engage in maritime security as land-based security issues are regarded as more urgent by most governments in East Africa.[81]

Summary

The previous sections have provided a comprehensive look at the commitments of governments in East and West Africa to combat insecurity at sea. Merely looking at documents such as the codes of conduct for both regions, however, is not enough. Regional organisations and the involvement—and interests—of outside actors also have to be considered to conduct a realistic analysis. None of the RECs in East and West Africa has a maritime focus, yet the established structures within those organisations are essential for political and practical efforts to improve maritime security.

Two aspects outlined in this chapter will be particularly important in the coming years. First and foremost, governments in many countries throughout both regions covered in this book have at least started to develop an interest in maritime issues generally and maritime security in particular, a positive sign after the maritime environment had not received much attention over the past decades. On the continental level, the *2050 AIM Strategy* is an important supplement to the AU's *Agenda 2063*, a long-term vision for a united and prosperous Africa.[82] On the regional level, agreements such as the two codes of conduct described in detail above show that it is possible to find common ground, even though governments may be concerned about a broad range of different maritime security issues on the national level.

Despite the unprecedented attention, maritime matters are still fairly low on the political agenda in most countries. Implementation of any measures, notably those announced in the context of both codes of conduct, will therefore remain challenging. Problems such as limited budgets for agencies with a maritime remit, a lack of navy ships that can operate at considerable distances from the coastline and a widespread shortage of maritime expertise are very unlikely to be resolved in the foreseeable future.

Secondly, existing institutional arrangements, notably within the RECs in East and West Africa, should be used to improve maritime security. Capacities within these organisations are limited, yet they offer a platform for further developments. Different centres for maritime cooperation in West Africa have been introduced in line with existing REC structures which are already used for cooperation to target land-based security threats. Agreements on the political as well as on the operational level are therefore much easier to find than within parallel or competing structures.

In East Africa, efforts to involve RECs to improve maritime security have been almost non-existent to date. International actors have shown a clear preference for short-term solutions related to counter-piracy operations in the western Indian Ocean. More recently, the focus has shifted to a broader view of maritime security issues, highlighted by discussions leading up to the DCoC amendment in 2017. Nevertheless, the long-term usefulness of donor-funded infrastructure and projects is highly doubtful. By and large, these will be 'unsustainable unless they result in a reduction of expenditures or an increase in government revenues'.[83]

Institutions cannot develop overnight. Lasting impacts are only possible when governments commit themselves to providing financial and human resources. While that is similar for virtually all challenges that countries in sub-Saharan Africa are facing, it is especially true when it comes to maritime questions which have been widely ignored for such a long time, despite the economic potential of the sea. In East Africa, problems are further amplified by the wide variety of signatories to the DCoC. Coastal states, archipelagic nations and Arab countries have vastly different interests and capabilities. Overall, however, it is much easier to take these into account when existing organisations offer a forum that has already helped to foster cooperation on other matters, even those that are completely unrelated to the maritime environment.

Notes

1. The Stable Seas Maritime Security Index provides a comprehensive overview over different issues linked to maritime security across sub-Saharan Africa and the implications on the national level; see Stable Seas. 2019. Maritime Security Index. One Earth Future Foundation. Available at: https://stableseas.org/maritime-security-index.
2. Tharoor, Ishan. 2009. How Somalia's fishermen became pirates. *Time*. Available at: http://content.time.com/time/world/article/0,8599,1892376,00.html.

3. No author. 2014. The ungoverned seas. *The Economist*. Available at: https://www.economist.com/middle-east-and-africa/2014/11/27/the-ungoverned-seas.
4. The complete documentary ‘Piracy in Nigeria’ was published on 17 November 2016 on Al Jazeera English’s Youtube channel. Available at: https://www.youtube.com/watch?v=866fXIAZsDk.
5. International Maritime Organization. *Barratry, unlawful seizure of ships and their cargoes and other forms of maritime fraud*. Resolution A. 504(XII), adopted on 20 November 1981 in London.
6. United Nations. 2019. Piracy and high seas crime growing, becoming more sophisticated, UN Security Council told. *UN News*. Available at: https://news.un.org/en/story/2019/02/1032011.
7. No author. 2011. Ghana Navy gets four armoured speedboats to protect offshore oil and gas installations. *Ghana Business News*. Available at: https://www.ghanabusinessnews.com/2011/10/24/ghana-navy-gets-four-armoured-speedboats-to-protect-offshore-oil-and-gas-installations/.
8. Reid, Cate. 2018. Mozambique: The anatomy of corruption. *The Africa Report*. Available at: https://www.theafricareport.com/607/mozambique-the-anatomy-of-corruption/.
9. Bousquet, Delphine. 2016. Benin’s anti-piracy fight gives maritime nation ‘life insurance’. *Modern Ghana*. Available at: https://www.modernghana.com/news/732279/benins-anti-piracy-fight-gives-maritime-nation-life-insura.html.
10. Blédé, Barthélémy and Diouf, André. *Togo’s maritime challenges: Why security remains a major issue*. Pretoria: Institute for Security Studies, 2016. Available at: https://issafrica.s3.amazonaws.com/site/uploads/WAR18_ENG.pdf.
11. For an overview of the problems caused by IUU fishing off Senegal, see, for example, Beatley, Meaghan and Edwards, Sam. 2018. Overfished: In Senegal, empty nets lead to hunger and violence. *Global Post Investigations*. Available at: https://gpinvestigations.pri.org/overfished-in-senegal-empty-nets-lead-to-hunger-and-violence-e3b5d0c9a686.
12. Bonnelame, Betymie. 2016. New coastal radar system means better safeguards for Seychelles, official says. *Seychelles News Agency*. Available at: http://www.seychellesnewsagency.com/articles/4828/New+coastal+radar+system+means+better+safeguards+for+Seychelles%2C+official+says.
13. For an overview over the role of armies throughout Africa, see Chuter, David and Gaub, Florence. *Understanding African armies*. Paris: EU Institute for Security Studies, 2016.
14. *NNS Thunder* (former US Coast Guard cutter *Chase*) and *NNS Okpabana* (former US Coast Guard cutter *Gallatin*).

15. No author. 2016. Nigeria gets $11m armoured vehicles from US to fight Boko Haram. *Business Day*. Available at: https://archive.businessday.ng/lagos/article/nigeria-gets-11m-armoured-vehicles-from-us-to-fight-boko-haram/.
16. US Coast Guard. 2018. International Acquisition Programs. Available at: https://www.dcms.uscg.mil/Portals/10/CG-9/Acquisition%20PDFs/Factsheets/FMS_FS.pdf?ver=2018-03-16-090604-910.
17. Other companies collect similar data but this company was chosen as an example of a commercial provider due to the authors affiliation with Risk Intelligence, providing easy access to relevant statistics. It should also be noted that based on the available sources and the requirements of clients, the interpretation of maritime security in West Africa can differ significantly across different companies and other organisations collecting similar data.
18. Examples include: Nincic, Donna. 2009. "Maritime piracy in Africa: The humanitarian dimension." *African Security Review*, Vol. 18:3. 2–5; Onuoha, Freedom C. 2010. "Piracy and Maritime Security off the Horn of Africa: Connections, causes and concerns." *African Security*, Vol. 3:4. 196–200; Anyimadu, Adjoa. *Maritime security in the Gulf of Guinea: Lessons learned from the Indian Ocean*. London: Chatham House, 2013. 4–5; Forster, Bruce A. 2014. "Modern maritime piracy: An overview of Somali Piracy, Gulf of Guinea Piracy and South East Asian Piracy." *British Journal of Economics, Management & Trade*, Vol. 4:8. 1258–1267; and Otto, Lisa. 2015. "Maritime crime in Nigeria and waters beyond analysing the period 2009 to 2013." *Africa Insight*, Vol. 45:1. 15–29.
19. Oceans Beyond Piracy. *The state of maritime piracy 2014*. Denver: One Earth Future Foundation, 2015. 37.
20. Personal interview with representative from shipping company, November 2018.
21. UNODC. *Somali Prison Survey Report: Piracy motivations & deterrents*, Report in cooperation with Oceans Beyond Piracy. Nairobi: UNODC, 2015.
22. See, for example, Obuah, Emmanuel. 2012. "Outsourcing the prosecution of Somali pirates to Kenya." *African Security Review*, Vol. 21:3. 40–61; Somers, Eduard. 2012. "The prosecution of alleged pirates: Is outsourcing the solution?" *Zanzibar Yearbook of Law*. 355–371.
23. One of the most prominent examples is the United Nations Office on Drugs and Crime's *Global Maritime Crime Programme—Atlantic Ocean*. An overview of activities since the start of the programme in 2014 is available at: https://www.unodc.org/unodc/en/piracy/atlantic-ocean.html.

24. Personal interview with representatives from several West African governments, November 2018.
25. N'Diaye, Boubacar. 2009. "Francophone Africa and Security Sector Transformation: Plus Ça Change." *African Security*, Vol. 2:1. 1–28.
26. Ghana's vessel traffic management information system, operated by the Ghana Maritime Authority, is a prime example. The system was commissioned in April 2014 to provide relevant agencies with a comprehensive picture of offshore activities. For a comprehensive discussion of the system, see Kuma, Joseph Akwasi. *Vessel traffic service as a maritime security tool: Vessel traffic management information systems (VTMIS) in Ghana*. Dissertation (MSc in Maritime Affairs). Malmö: World Maritime University, 2015.
27. The Kenyan government even created a new coastguard in November 2018; see Mwakio, Philip. 2018. Uhuru unveils Kenya Coast Guard Service. *Standard Digital*. Available at: https://www.standardmedia.co.ke/article/2001303305/uhuru-unveils-kenya-coast-guard-service.
28. Holihead, Philip. 2013. *Building on existing codes of conduct to promote regional cooperation for all aspects of maritime development—An opportunity not to be missed*. Third UAE Counter Piracy Conference, Briefing Paper. 1.
29. The official title of the document, *Code of Conduct concerning the repression of piracy and armed robbery against ships in the Western Indian Ocean and the Gulf of Aden*, clearly shows its narrow focus.
30. Personal interview with representative from the International Maritime Organization, May 2014. During the meeting in Djibouti that was held to adopt the original code in 2009, a specific resolution on technical cooperation and assistance was also passed, requesting contributions from individual countries and international organisations to support the implementation of the code.
31. Dutton, Yvonne M. 2011. "Pirates and impunity: Is the threat of asylum claims a reason to allow pirates to escape justice?" *Fordham International Law Journal*, Vol. 34:2. 240–241.
32. Japan set up a military base in Djibouti in 2009 after the government had provided funding for a regional training centre in the country through the International Maritime Organization. The base was linked to the fight against Somalia-based pirates, but it also provided the country with a strategic presence in the region. In 2018, an extension was announced: Ryall, Julian. 2018. Japan do expand Djibouti base despite decline in piracy. *Deutsche Welle*. Available at: https://www.dw.com/en/japan-to-expand-djibouti-base-despite-decline-in-piracy/a-46356825. In 2014, the US military had already renewed the lease for its base at Camp Lemonnier for which it now pays around US$70 million per year

to Djibouti's government. Plans for significant upgrades to the base were announced at the same time: Wood, Josh. 2015. Djibouti, a safe harbour in the troubled Horn of Africa. *The National.* Available at: https://www.thenational.ae/world/djibouti-a-safe-harbour-in-the-troubled-horn-of-africa-1.96706.

33. Dabugat, Kop'ep. *African approaches to maritime security: The West and Central African perspectives.* Report of the international conference organised by the Friedrich-Ebert-Stiftung in collaboration with the National Defence College, Abuja, 21–23 May 2014.
34. International Maritime Organization. *Code of Conduct concerning the repression of piracy, armed robbery against ships, and illicit maritime activity in West and Central Africa.* Signed in Yaoundé on 25 June 2013. 4. Available at: http://www.imo.org/en/OurWork/Security/WestAfrica/Documents/code_of_conduct%20signed%20from%20ECOWAS%20site.pdf.
35. Ukeje, Charles and Mvomo Ela, Wullson. *African approaches to maritime security—The Gulf of Guinea.* Abuja: Friedrich-Ebert-Stiftung, 2013. 36–39.
36. International Maritime Organization. *Code of Conduct (…) West and Central Africa.* 5.
37. Kraska, James. "Looking for law in all the wrong places: Maritime piracy as a domestic legal problem." Briefing paper for *Global challenge, regional responses: Forging a common approach to maritime piracy.* Conference in Dubai, UAE on 18 and 19 April 2011. 105–106.
38. Guilfoyle, Douglas. "Towards a robust legal framework on piracy: Law and politics." Briefing paper for *Global challenge, regional responses: Forging a common approach to maritime piracy.* Conference in Dubai, UAE on 18 and 19 April 2011. 97–98.
39. Personal interview with representative of government ministry in West Africa, November 2017.
40. International Maritime Organization. 2017. *Revised Code of Conduct concerning the repression of piracy, armed robbery against ships, and illicit maritime activity in the western Indian Ocean and the Gulf of Aden area.* Adopted in Jeddah, Saudi Arabia on 12 January 2017. Available at: http://www.imo.org/en/OurWork/Security/PIU/Documents/DCOC%20Jeddah%20Amendment%20English.pdf.
41. Syrén, Hakan. *Keynote speech: Bridging efforts—Connecting civilian security and military capability development.* Brussels: European Defence Agency, 2009. 7.
42. Davidson, Basil. *Africa in history: Themes and outlines (revised and expanded edition).* London: Orion Books, 1992. 351.

43. African Union. 2019. Constitutive Act. Available at: https://au.int/en/constitutive-act.
44. For a general introduction of the role played by regional economic institutions in peacekeeping on the African continent, see Brosig, Malte. *Cooperative peacekeeping in Africa—Exploring regime complexity*. London: Routledge, 2015. Chapter 5 analyses the role of regional economic communities in particular.
45. Discussed comprehensively by Konings (2011).
46. Oduntan, Gbenga. 2015. Africa's border disputes are set to rise—But there are ways to stop them. *Defence Web*. Available at: https://www.defenceweb.co.za/security/border-security/africas-border-disputes-are-set-to-rise-but-there-are-ways-to-stop-them/?catid=87%3Aborder-security&Itemid=188.
47. Opalo, Ken. 2010. The Ogaden Region: Fragile path to peace. *Africa Portal*. Available at: https://www.africaportal.org/publications/the-ogaden-region-a-fragile-path-to-peace/.
48. African Union. 2013. The 387th Peace and Security Council meeting supports the call by the Yaoundé summit to elaborate and adopt a regional strategy in line with the AU 2050 AIM-Strategy. Available at: https://au.int/fr/node/27467.
49. Bagayoko, Niagalé. *Security systems in francophone Africa*. IDS Research Report 64. Brighton: Institute of Development Studies at the University of Sussex, 2010. 54–66.
50. Personal interviews with representatives of government agencies from different countries in East and West Africa, June 2014 to November 2018.
51. Economic Community of West African States. *Revised treaty of the Economic Community of West African States (ECOWAS)*. Opened for signature on 24 July 1993.
52. Adebajo 2002 provides a comprehensive summary.
53. The overall concept and the development of the African Standby Force have been discussed in detail by different authors. Notable examples include: Cilliers, Jakkie. *The African Standby Force: An update on progress*. ISS Paper 160. Pretoria: Institute for Security Studies, 2008; Dersso, Solomon A. *The role and place of the African Standby Force within the African Peace and Security Architecture*. ISS Paper 209. Pretoria: Institute for Security Studies, 2010; and Darkwa, Linda. 2017. "The African Standby Force: The African Union's tool for the maintenance of peace and security." *Contemporary Security Policy*, Vol. 38:3. 471–482.
54. Communauté économique des États de l'Afrique Centrale. *Treaty establishing the Economic Community of Central African States*. Opened for signature on 18 October 1983.

55. Personal interviews with representatives of the navies from Cameroon and Equatorial Guinea, April 2016.
56. United Nations. 2011. *Regional confidence-building measures: Activities of the United Nations Standing Advisory Committee on Security Questions in Central Africa: Report of the Secretary General.* 9.
57. Personal interviews with representatives of the navies from Cameroon and Equatorial Guinea, April 2016.
58. United Nations Security Council. 2012. *Report of the United Nations assessment mission on piracy in the Gulf of Guinea* (7 to 24 November 2011). 13. Available at: http://www.securitycouncilreport.org/atf/cf/%7B65BFCF9B-6D27-4E9C-8CD3-CF6E4FF96FF9%7D/AUUN%20S%202012%2045.pdf.
59. Similar issues have been identified for the security cooperation among ECCAS members; see Meyer, Angela. *Peace and security cooperation in Central Africa.* Discussion Paper 56. Uppsala: Nordiska Afrikainstitutet, 2011.
60. Ploch, Blanchard, O'Rourke et al. *Piracy off the Horn of Africa.* Washington, DC: Congressional Research Service, 2011. 23.
61. United Nations Office on Drugs and Crime. 2019. Maritime Crime Programme—Horn of Africa. Available at: https://www.unodc.org/unodc/en/piracy/horn-of-africa-division.html.
62. See, for example, Adar, Korwa G. 2000. "Conflict resolution in a turbulent region: The case of the Intergovernmental Authority on Development (IGAD) in Sudan." *African Journal on Conflict Resolution*, Vol. 1:2. 39–66; Terlinden, Ulf. *IGAD—Paper tiger facing gigantic tasks.* Berlin: Friedrich-Ebert-Stiftung, 2004; and Sousa, Ricardo Real P. 2013. "African Peace and Security Architecture (APSA) subsidiarity and the Horn of Africa: The Intergovernmental Authority on Development (IGAD)." In: *State and societal challenges in the Horn of Africa: Conflict and processes of state formation, reconfiguration and disintegration.* Lisbon: CEA. 59–77.
63. Personal interview with representative from East African government, June 2017.
64. Elowson, Camilla and Lins de Albuquerque, Adriana. 2016. Challenges to peace and security in Eastern Africa: The fole of IGAD, EAC and EASF. Swedish Research Agency. Available at: https://www.foi.se/download/18.7fd35d7f166c56ebe0bb38e/1542369060243/Challenges-to-Peace-and-Security-in-Eastern-Africa_FOI-Memo-5634.pdf.
65. For a detailed analysis on the success of trade agreements and the removal of non-trade barriers within the EAC, see Kimbugwe, Perkidis, Yeung and Kerr. *Economic development through regional trade—A role for the new East African Community?* Basingstoke: Palgrave Macmillan, 2012.

66. Martinez, Jorge Bolanos. 2012. Joint military exercises in Rwanda: Towards a new security and defense architecture in East Africa. Instituto Espanol de Estudios Estratégicos. Available at: http://www.ieee.es/en/Galerias/fichero/docs_informativos/2012/DIEEEI67-2012_ManiobrasMilitares_JBM_ENGLISH.pdf.
67. Elowson, Camilla and Lins de Albuquerque, Adriana. 2016. Challenges to peace and security in Eastern Africa.
68. Missiroli, Antonio and Popowski, Maciej. "Foreword." In: Tardy, Thierry (ed.) *Fighting piracy off the coast of Somalia—Lessons learned from the Contact Group*. Report No. 20. Paris: EU Institute for Security Studies, 2014. 3.
69. Personal interview with retired flag officer and former member of CTF 151 staff, May 2016.
70. Tardy, Thierry (ed.) *Fighting piracy off the coast of Somalia*.
71. Gaas, Mohamed Husein. "A Somali perspective on the Contact Group." In: Tardy, Thierry (ed.) *Fighting piracy off the coast of Somalia—Lessons learned from the Contact Group*. Report No. 20. Paris: EU Institute for Security Studies, 2014. 71–77.
72. Amla, Hajira. 2014. Seychelles receives $6.4m in sustainable development and climate change grants from EU. *Seychelles News Agency*. Available at: http://www.seychellesnewsagency.com/articles/1875/Seychelles+receives+.m+in+sustainable+development+and+climate+change+grants+from+EU.
73. Walsh, Michael Edward. 2017. Djibouti: IMO recommends transforming training center. CPD Blog. Available at: https://www.uscpublicdiplomacy.org/blog/djibouti-imo-recommends-transforming-training-center.
74. Ryall, Julian. 2018. Japan do expand Djibouti base despite decline in piracy.
75. For a detailed map of the originally planned structure with three different information fusion centres, see Oceans Beyond Piracy. 2014. Information sharing in the western Indian Ocean. Available at: http://oceansbeyondpiracy.org/sites/default/files/attachments/EastAfricaInfoSharingMap.pdf.
76. No author. 2017. MASE Programme, a regional response to maritime insecurity. IGAD. Available at: https://igad.int/divisions/peace-and-security/1552-mase-programme-a-regional-response-to-maritime-insecurity.
77. Ilioniaina, Alain. 2015. Madagascar: un centre d'informations maritimes, planchet de salut contre la piraterie. *Anadolu Agency*. Available at: https://www.aa.com.tr/fr/politique/madagascar-un-centre-dinformations-maritimes-planche-de-salut-contre-la-piraterie/43725.

78. At the time of writing, only five countries (France [Reunion], Comoros, Djibouti, Madagascar and Seychelles) had agreed to take part in the RCOC; see No author. 2018. EU ambassador Marjaana Sall visits centre. *Seychelles Nation*. Available at: http://www.nation.sc/article.html?id=259328.
79. No author. 2019. The IORIS Platform. EU CRIMARIO. Available at: https://www.crimario.eu/en/information-sharing/the-ioris-platform/.
80. Personal interviews with naval officers and government representatives from various countries in East and West Africa, June 2014 to March 2019.
81. See, for example, Witt, Antonia. *10th FES annual conference: Peace and security in the Horn of Africa*. Nairobi, 21–22 October 2014. Available at: http://library.fes.de/pdf-files/bueros/aethiopien/11552-20150807.pdf; Shaban, Abdur Rahman Alfa. 2016. Al-Shabab is a threat to East Africa region—IGAD report. *Africa News*. Available at: https://www.africanews.com/2016/08/16/al-shabab-is-a-threat-to-east-africa-region-igad/.
82. African Union. *Agenda 2063: The Africa we want*. Addis Ababa: African Union, 2015.
83. No author. *Ships, guns, but no laws? Whitepaper on piracy in the Gulf of Guinea*. Hellerup: Risk Intelligence. 7.

CHAPTER 6

Contrasting Regions

Abstract Drawing on the research presented throughout the previous parts of the book, this chapter shows essential differences between East and West Africa which need to be noted in discussions about maritime security. At the same time, both regions share some key characteristics, for example the impact of illegal, unreported and unregulated (IUU) fishing throughout territorial waters and the exclusive economic zones (EEZ) on coastal communities and a focus of outside actors that is often limited to piracy and armed robbery at sea. These similar traits create opportunities to draw on lessons learned, both on the national and on the regional level. The chapter also explains that neither East nor West Africa are likely to develop into a genuine maritime security complex or even a maritime security community. Nevertheless, maritime challenges may provide an impetus for enhanced cooperation within existing regional security complexes in both regions. Finally, the chapter provides recommendations that would help to secure sustainable improvements of maritime security. These are aimed at four specific sets of actors: governments in East and West Africa, their international partners, non-governmental organisations and the private sector.

Keywords Territorial waters · EEZ · Maritime security community · Regional security complex · Recommendations

D. Siebels, *Maritime Security in East and West Africa*,
https://doi.org/10.1007/978-3-030-22688-6_6

Various issues related to maritime security in East and West Africa that were outlined in the previous chapters show that both regions are facing similar problems, yet the responses over the past decade have been very different. Arguably, the best starting points for a comprehensive discussion are the two different codes of conduct, including the development of the Djibouti Code of Conduct (DCoC) to a document that is concerned with a broad range of maritime security issues.

Originally, it had taken governments in West Africa several more years to agree on a code of conduct after such a document had been adopted in East Africa as early as 2009. Additional time for negotiations, however, was well spent, leading to a document that was much more comprehensive than the DCoC which was solely concerned with piracy and armed robbery at sea until it was finally amended in 2017. Both codes of conduct are now all-encompassing documents and provide solid frameworks to address regional security challenges in the maritime environment. They may even become standards for other regions around the world, even though it remains to be seen whether the measures stipulated in the documents can be implemented in practice.

In the context of limited budgets and a widespread lack of political will, both codes of conduct are remarkable achievements. Governments across East and West Africa have neglected maritime issues for decades before finally starting to discuss these challenges. Security efforts remain concentrated on land, yet West Africa in particular has benefited from an established regional framework within the regional economic communities (RECs) Economic Community of West African States (ECOWAS) and—to a lesser extent—Economic Community of Central African States (ECCAS). Both organisations may lack internal cohesion[1] and have a limited track record for security cooperation, but established procedures and relationships have already proved to be a stepping stone for an increasing amount of cooperation related to maritime security.[2]

Similar arrangements are hard to identify in East Africa. While the lower number of countries compared to West Africa would suggest that it is easier to find common ground, 'divergent country attitudes towards regional integration'[3] have been a long-standing problem. Economic integration has been a contentious political topic in the past, and any security-related debates provide further challenges due to the implications on national sovereignty.[4]

For both regions, it is important to find sustainable solutions which are very unlikely to be implemented within just a few years.

The involvement of international actors, particularly in East Africa, will not provide much assistance as long as it is based on their political agendas rather than priorities within the region itself. Long-term funding is another aspect that needs to be addressed.

Based on the research outlined in the previous chapters, the following sections will look at the development of efforts to improve regional maritime security in East and West Africa. It can be used as a baseline for further research on related topics as well as a blueprint for similar academic projects in other regions around the world. The final section includes a list of recommendations for different actors, highlighting at least some of the actions that are necessary to improve maritime security in the years to come.

6.1 Comparison Between East and West Africa

In recent years, the potential of the blue economy as a cornerstone for economic development has been mentioned in an increasing number of speeches, policy papers and media articles. With the adoption of the *2050 AIM Strategy* in 2014, the African Union (AU) became a key advocate of the concept. It should be noted that the strategy contains a number of highly ambitious goals, for example a Combined Exclusive Maritime Zone of Africa which would require governments to give up an important part of sovereign national rights in the maritime environment. Nevertheless, the document underlines that African leaders have at least started to consider the negative impact of insecurity at sea on growth and development on land.

Implementation of day-to-day measures, however, remains largely dependent on national governments and, perhaps more importantly, RECs across the African continent. Unfortunately, resources for any additional measures are severely limited, leading to bottlenecks both on the political and on the operational levels. At the same time, AU experts know that the eventual success of any maritime policy depends on practical measures on the REC level, summarised by an AU official: 'Without the RECs, we are nothing. We can sit down and write papers in Addis all day but somebody has to translate them into something practical. We have to work as African brothers, not just within the borders imposed on us by our colonial masters'.[5]

These problems have been underlined once again by a lack of action on important parts of the Lomé Charter, notably the planned creation of a continent-wide fund for maritime safety and security. The charter was adopted during an international summit in the Togolese capital in 2016, intended as another step towards fulfilling the *2050 AIM Strategy*'s goals.[6] Most signatories, however, have so far failed to agree on integrated maritime strategies on the national level, even though such documents are urgently needed 'to improve synergy between these strategies and those set up at regional and continental level'.[7]

On the regional level, East and West Africa show some similarities, but also important differences when it comes to the perception of the 'blue economy' in general and maritime security in particular. Offshore oil and gas production, for example, has long been established throughout West Africa while it is still a fledgling industry in East Africa where it is largely limited to Mozambique and Tanzania. Negative impacts of illegal, unreported and unregulated (IUU) fishing, on the other hand, can be felt in coastal communities across both regions.

Overall, the analysis of similarities and differences is important when maritime strategies are discussed or updated, both on the regional and on the national levels. Resources to improve maritime security are generally scarce and have to be used in areas with a good cost–benefit ratio. When the use of additional resources has the potential to create immediate benefits for governments and the overall population, opposition against such measures is much more likely to be overcome. Some lessons can be learned from looking at other countries or regions, but their maritime strategies can only be a rough template in this respect. Specific issues and requirements have to be taken into account as well; there is no 'one-size-fits-all' type of maritime strategy.

Essential Differences

One of the most important differences between both regions is the established REC structures in West Africa with ECOWAS and—on a more limited scale—ECCAS already involved in security cooperation, including joint military missions. Moreover, Nigeria can be described as a regional hegemon. The country has by far the largest population and the largest economy in the region as well as significant military capabilities which can be a blessing and a curse at the same time. On the one hand, the Nigerian government can stimulate other governments to act. On the other hand, many West Africans are wary of too much Nigerian influence in all political areas.

East Africa does not have a similarly dominant country. While Ethiopia has the largest military[8] and the largest population, the Kenyan GDP is almost exactly the same size, despite a much smaller population.[9] There are also fewer countries than in West Africa with a coastline, maritime matters therefore play only a minor role in East Africa's established RECs. Finally, these RECs are less developed when it comes to cooperation in the security sector and there are no genuinely regional initiatives related to maritime security. The Djibouti Code of Conduct in its amended version has the potential to become a comprehensive framework for regional initiatives related to maritime security, yet it remains to be seen whether governments in East Africa are indeed willing to adopt a more proactive role.

Past experiences with the implementation of the DCoC after its original adoption in 2009 are a good example for the complicated cooperation between international partners and regional governments. Somalia-based piracy has long been considered as the primary—if not the only—maritime security concern in East Africa from an international point of view, leading to various naval operations as well as technical and financial assistance for related initiatives across East Africa. More often than not, these were not based on regional requirements, leading to question marks regarding the long-term sustainability of training facilities or information-sharing centres.

West Africa has not experienced a similar inflow of financial assistance to create new infrastructure. There are examples of international partners providing assistance for tasks related to maritime security, yet such programmes are largely limited to workshops, training programmes and other forms of capability development.[10] Policymakers and practitioners alike should avoid the pitfalls of externally funded infrastructure which may lead to recurring expenses that governments are unwilling or unable to pay.

Another key difference between East and West Africa is the structure of the shipping industry. Maritime traffic patterns are important on the operational level because maritime situational awareness requires different technical measures. In West Africa, coastal radar stations with a range of 20–30 nautical miles are enough to provide security agencies with information about a large proportion of maritime traffic which is concentrated around ports and anchorages. Cooperation with companies involved in offshore oil and gas production can further expand the capabilities of maritime agencies.

In East Africa, however, most countries have relatively long coastlines and a limited amount of maritime traffic close to the coastline, requiring aerial or satellite surveillance systems to keep track of important patterns. At the same time, there is no established offshore industry in the region which could at least help to alleviate the lack of maritime situational awareness.

Finally, the involvement of private companies in the provision of maritime security should be mentioned. In East Africa, the private sector originally started to take part in the fight against Somalia-based piracy through the provision of armed guards on merchant ships. Some of these companies tried to introduce the same business model in West Africa where piracy and armed robbery at sea have long been problems for ship operators.

Coastal states in West Africa, however, do not tolerate privately contracted armed security personnel on merchant ships in their territorial waters, leading to different forms of public–private partnerships. The most interesting model has developed in Nigeria where private companies are operating patrol boats that are partly manned by naval personnel and contracted by oil companies or ship operators to provide additional security for their assets. Such partnerships, possibly extending to other tasks, may be an opportunity for governments in both East and West Africa to quickly improve the capacities of navies and other agencies with a maritime remit and should therefore be studied very closely.

Similarities in Both Regions

Pirate attacks against merchant ships have arguably been the most headline-grabbing issue related to maritime security in East and West Africa over the past decade. Other aspects, notably IUU fishing, have received much less public, academic and political attention, even though the impact may be much greater, particularly on the domestic level. By and large, the economic burden of IUU fishing has to be shouldered by the artisanal fishing sector in poor countries. Mere calculations of absolute costs are therefore misleading as even relatively small sums can have a devastating impact on coastal communities where fishing is the main economic activity for most families.

Moreover, IUU fishing is a genuine maritime security problem that could impact security on land in the medium term, for example through economic migration away from coastal communities. Piracy and armed robbery at sea, on the other hand, are merely symptoms of instability on land which leads to a permissive environment for such activities.[11]

Thoroughly analysing attacks against merchant ships is nevertheless important. Piracy-related headlines are important to create at least some political attention for maritime security issues. Such attacks may have other implications as well, increasing the costs of maritime trade and therefore undermining the ongoing efforts to strengthen the blue economy. Unfortunately, some areas may be wrongly identified as hotspots for pirate attacks, highlighted by the discussion of different sets of statistics about such incidents in Chapter 5.

The limited focus on piracy on armed robbery at sea, largely caused by lobbying from the directly affected shipping industry and amplified by outside governments and international organisations, is frequently criticised in East and West Africa. In Somalia, the hijacking of merchant ships became a lucrative business model but the origins of piracy are widely perceived as self-defence against IUU fishing[12] and the dumping of toxic waste at sea.[13] While these issues are no justification for attacks against merchant ships passing through the western Indian Ocean, it is at least somewhat ironic that European and Asian governments sent warships to combat Somali pirates after they failed to prevent fishing vessels plundering fish stocks off the Somali coastline.[14]

In West Africa, there is also a general feeling that the threat of piracy is exaggerated by outside actors. The former Director General of the Nigerian Maritime Administration and Safety Agency (NIMASA) even said that 'most of the reported piracy attacks [in sub-Saharan Africa] are untrue and a deliberate sabotage from foreign insurance companies'.[15] In 2018, his successor made similar claims, albeit in a slightly more understated manner.[16] Figures about pirate attacks published by NIMASA suggest that the number of attacks against all types of ships off Nigeria's coastline is extremely limited, despite even the Nigerian Navy painting a very different picture.[17] The disconnect is mainly due to inter-agency rivalries on the domestic level, highlighting an important hurdle on the long way to a more secure environment at sea.

At the same time, the example serves as a reminder that piracy should not be prioritised over other challenges that are solely domestic concerns. 'We have many criminals on land, but we don't deal with them properly. Sometimes they will attack ships, but that is a headline in European newspapers. When the same people rob a Cameroonian on his way to the port, nobody will care about it'.[18] Such opinions may not be received well by foreign donors, yet they should be taken into account to create sustainable solutions. Resources are likely to be wasted when domestic populations are unable to see the benefits of better maritime security. Tangible benefits such as an increase in employment opportunities, on the other hand, can help to convince government representatives that investments in the maritime environment are worthwhile.

Changes in the perception of the 'blue economy' are already afoot. In 2014, the foreign minister of the Seychelles stated that 'there is a need to change the relationship with the ocean from one of purely extraction to one of development (…) [but] many African coastal states lack the capacity to manage their oceanic territory and exclusive economic zones'.[19] The UN's Economic Commission for Africa then published a policy handbook on Africa's blue economy in 2016, intended to help in the 'pursuit of structural transformation, sustainable economic growth, and enduring societal progress'.[20] Kenya's government ensured further attention for the topic by hosting the *Sustainable Blue Economy Conference* in November 2018. It was the first global conference on the topic, bringing more than 18,000 participants to Nairobi.[21]

Aside from these positive developments, corruption should also be mentioned as a challenge that affects maritime security in both East and West Africa. Corrupt practices 'dog the development of the [maritime] industry'[22] and undermine trust in government agencies. An example from Nigeria shows the extent of facilitation payments requested from ships calling at ports in the country: 'Frequent demands were made by Immigration, Environmental Authorities, Health Inspectors, Quarantine Office, Customs, National Port Authorities and National Drug Law Enforcement Agency'.[23] In most other countries across both regions, similar practices are also widespread and 'corruption is so integral to certain aspects of governance that anti-corruption initiatives are likely to meet resistance from politicians as well as civil servants'.[24]

At the same time, personnel working for agencies with a maritime remit is often unable to conduct their regular tasks. Fishing vessels, for example, may be detained for illegal practices but are later released after what is often described as 'a call from above', meaning an order from superior officers, government officials or politicians.[25]

Corruption is a wide-ranging problem that is not an exclusive challenge in the maritime environment. The international character of most activities related to the blue economy, however, creates a somewhat unique situation. On the one hand, foreigners may even profit from perceived corruption problems. Captains on many merchant vessels calling at West African ports, for example, are suspected to inflate unofficial payments in reports to their company offices in a bid to keep some of the money for themselves.[26] On the other hand, cooperation between African agencies and external partners is often complicated by corrupt practices,[27] leading to a vicious circle that makes it even harder for security agencies to conduct their day-to-day tasks.

6.2 Maritime Security Complex or Maritime Security Community?

Some definitions of regional security complexes in sub-Saharan Africa by Buzan and Wæver were discussed in Chapter 2. Whether these definitions, originally made in 2003, are still valid is an interesting debate which is beyond the scope of this book. It is important to note, however, that the academic debate related to this topic has generally been focused on land-based security challenges.[28]

By and large, maritime security is not a vital issue for governments. Even a relatively broad range of threats in the maritime environment has a limited influence on the boundaries of any regional security complex in Africa. Most maritime security threats are transnational, yet they are mostly symptoms of land-based issues, for example bad governance or weak law enforcement. Instead of trying to create an artificial maritime security complex, issues in the maritime environment should be addressed within existing regional security complexes where cooperation may already exist on some levels. It may even support cooperation when neighbouring countries find a maritime security threat such as piracy or IUU fishing as a common denominator that helps to build trust and establish joint decision-making.

In academic discussions related to security politics, there has been an increasing focus on specific regions over the past years. This can be linked to three key factors[29]:

- security threats are rarely contained within the borders of any country;
- partnerships between the international community and regional organisations have become increasingly important in the context

of interventions that are conducted within the region but partly sponsored by outside actors;
- many regional organisations—not only in Africa—are trying to take a more proactive role in addressing security threats.

Any regional security complex is mainly defined by geography. '[T]hreats travel more easily over short distances than over long ones'[30] and, by extension, governments simply have to accept that they are part of such a complex where security is influenced by events in neighbouring countries. According to Buzan and Wæver, four aspects define the structure of regional security complexes[31]:

- more or less distinct geographic boundaries;
- patterns of amity or enmity among individual units;
- distribution of power between individual unit;
- anarchic structure within the entire security complex.

Developing a security complex into a security community is a voluntary process, requiring at least some cooperation on the governmental level to overcome the anarchic structure. Europe is arguably the best example for a security community which has developed in different steps after the end of the Second World War.[32] It shows that state actions within a security community are largely based on processes of norm construction, socialisation, rational behaviour and social learning. Another significant contrast to realist approaches is the perception of security which is not only based on the interests, but also on the identity of a state.[33]

Common institutions are widespread in different policy areas in Europe. The situation in Africa is extremely different. By and large, state-level cooperation is weak, yet cultural, historic and linguistic links encourage informal cross-border networks and relations. The development of ECOWAS in West Africa is an interesting example in this respect. The organisation deployed a peacekeeping force in Liberia as early as 1990 and has faced a range of common threats since, leading to discussions about the evolution of a security community in West Africa.[34] Cooperation, however, is often complicated by a lack of financial resources and qualified personnel. On the regional level, 'institutional frameworks exist (…) [but] not many practical initiatives have taken place',[35] highlighting the challenges that governments in the region still have to master.

Other regional organisations on the African continent such as ECCAS, Intergovernmental Authority on Development (IGAD) or the East African Community (EAC) are facing similar or even greater constraints. Nevertheless, these organisations are quintessential actors in the fight against transnational security threats, including those in the maritime environment. They are recognised by the African Union, have created at least some institutional capacities and therefore provide a platform to develop and implement long-term strategies.

Creating additional institutions might have short-term benefits from the perspective of foreign partners and donors. In the long term, however, there is nothing to suggest that African governments will be able to support such institutions when financial and human resources are not even enough to fully equip the existing RECs. While that is a general issue, efforts to address Somali piracy largely failed to take into account existing institutions, leading to an institutional framework that continues to rely heavily on assistance from outside the region.[36]

Positive effects of joint operations or trainings and information-sharing are key aspects in the bottom-up development of any security community.[37] Cooperation on the operational level, however, has to be supported by efforts on the overarching political level. In this context, maritime security challenges may better be regarded as a subset of overall regional challenges, not only those in the security sector. Similar to specific land-based security threats, small nations may be disproportionately affected and can concentrate their efforts on particular issues. The high-profile role of the Seychelles in counter-piracy activities and outspoken support from the Togolese government for the AU's maritime strategy are good examples.

Overall, none of the maritime security challenges discussed in this book are the potential foundation of a genuine maritime security community. Maritime issues such as piracy and armed robbery at sea, IUU fishing, smuggling or illegal migration are all linked to land-based problems, including—but not limited to—bad governance and weak law enforcement. Enhanced cooperation between maritime security agencies is therefore important to address these issues and to strengthen ties within both East and West Africa. However, enhanced cooperation is much more likely to be sustainable when it takes place within existing institutions, namely the regional economic communities. The ongoing—albeit slow—implementation of the Yaoundé Code of Conduct in West Africa is a good example for efforts that are likely to be sustainable in the long term.

6.3 Recommendations for Different Actors

Insecurity at sea, as pointed out in the previous chapters, is merely one symptom of more general issues, both on the regional and on the national levels. Most countries in Africa have 'failed to manage the industries that partly or fully operate at sea, guarantee the socio-economic welfare of coastal communities or enforce the law in territorial or international waters',[38] caused by a combination of limited human and financial resources and a lack of political will to improve governance in the maritime environment. It will require long-term efforts in a range of areas to improve maritime security and to create a solid foundation for a flourishing blue economy.

Different actors need to act together to address most of these issues. Corruption, for example, is a far-reaching problem that affects countries in East and West Africa in many policy areas. It is therefore impossible to address corruption only as far as it influences maritime security. Nevertheless, the shipping industry may be able to act decisively, reduce corruption and therefore create a positive example for other areas.

Limited resources for navies or maritime law enforcement agencies are another aspect that should not be addressed in isolation. Security agencies on land often face similar resource constraints, and it is hardly expedient to provide additional funding or personnel merely to improve maritime security rather than strengthen the security sector overall. At the same time, the unique characteristics of maritime security may offer potential for public–private partnerships which could help governments to create a short-term solution for capacity constraints.

Such overarching issues are important, yet there are many aspects that could help to improve maritime security significantly in both East and West Africa. Politicians, academics and practitioners should look closely at lessons learned from projects and experiences in either region. The following paragraphs include various recommendations for different stakeholders in the maritime environment, including governments, international partners, non-governmental organisations and the private sector.

Governments in East and West Africa

Transporting goods on maritime routes to and from countries in sub-Saharan Africa is more expensive than in other world regions, explained in detail in Chapter 3. Insecurity at sea only has a very limited direct impact on the overall transport costs which are more likely to be influenced by the size and efficiency of ports or hinterland connections. Decisions about large-scale infrastructure investments, however, are certainly not encouraged by—real or perceived—gaps in maritime security, making it even harder to leverage maritime trade routes for the overall economic development of any country.

Governments, therefore, need to act on multiple layers. On the national level, comprehensive maritime strategies are vital to ensure that any future efforts and investments are part of an overarching structure. Maritime security is only one component of any broader maritime strategy, yet it is a key part when it comes to cooperation with international partners and attracting investments from the private sector.[39]

Providing additional resources to maritime agencies may be useful, but improved cooperation between different agencies and a clear focus on specific tasks can also yield very positive results. National governments should therefore conduct a thorough cost–benefit analysis to identify those areas where efforts of security agencies create the highest returns. That will help to create a situation where the economic potential of the maritime environment can be exploited to the benefit of national economies and coastal communities, leading in turn to additional support for the implementation of necessary efforts.

On the regional level, governments should cooperate within existing fora such as the RECs in East and West Africa. National maritime strategies may be notably different even in neighbouring countries, based on aspects like geography, economic factors like fishing patterns or hydrocarbon reserves, and political influence of specific groups. Such differences are unavoidable but should not be perceived as a stumbling block to improved bilateral and multilateral coordination. Cooperation should rather be based on identifying common challenges and the fact that most actions related to maritime security in one country can lead to an unwanted impact on neighbouring countries.

Another aspect is often highlighted by international partners, namely the ability to prosecute piracy and armed robbery at sea. While that may indeed be a challenge in some countries, it is rarely due to the lack of necessary laws. Changing or creating relevant laws merely at the behest of foreign donors is therefore not expedient. Based on a comprehensive maritime strategy, it is relatively simple to identify actual areas of concern, for example a lack of qualified prosecutors or other shortcomings in the judicial system. These shortcomings can then be targeted and addressed as part of the implementation of strategic goals on the national level rather than based on political priorities of partners from outside the region.

International Partners

Arguably, the most high-profile involvement of external partners in both regions discussed throughout this book has been related to the fight against Somalia-based piracy. Most counter-piracy initiatives, however, were supposed to provide short-term solutions rather than sustainable improvements of maritime security overall across the western part of the Indian Ocean. The focus only started to shift in recent years, highlighted by the amended version of the DCoC. Regional cohesion, however, is complicated by the fact that existing regional organisations have rarely been part of the relevant discussions, thus leaving them with little say during the implementation of projects related to maritime security.

Efforts in West Africa show that such projects are usually a long-term challenge. The same can be said for developing cross-border cooperation among governments and relevant agencies. At the same time, ongoing improvements should provide external partners with an impression of potential. Developing a comprehensive approach to improve maritime security may be complicated after the topic had been largely ignored for decades, yet it is possible.

At the same time, international partners are often looking for short-term success rather than long-term progress, leading some authors to recommend bilateral pilot projects 'guided by a return on investment methodology that takes into account security threat and consequences, the receptivity of the country to assistance, its ability to absorb the assistance and its willingness and capability to politically and financially sustain the effort for the long term'.[40] Such an idea, however, fails to address the fact that the return on investment may be calculated from different perspectives or that consequences of security threats are highly diverse across different stakeholders. The hijacking of a merchant vessel, for example, has severe consequences for the crew and the owner of the ship, yet may be beneficial for coastal communities if the threat level leads to less IUU fishing in the respective area.

When international partners get involved solely based on their own agendas, efforts are unlikely to be based on requirements of government agencies in East and West Africa. Creating solutions that are sustainable in the long term requires international partners to exert pressure on regional governments to act by themselves. Assistance can then be provided for clearly identified requirements, based on an overarching maritime strategy and long-term goals for the blue economy.

International partners should also ensure compliance with their own laws and regulations. Corruption is a prime example. International governments often single out corruption as a major obstacle across many political areas in general, but it also has an impact on maritime security in particular. At the same time, these governments have rarely started to act to ensure compliance with their own laws or to prevent domestic companies from paying bribes abroad to secure large contracts.[41] This type of hypocritical behaviour is hardly limited to the maritime environment, yet the international character of industries such as energy or shipping provides international partners with broad potential for the prevention of suspect or criminal practices.

Coordination of assistance by international partners should also be improved. Various agencies from the EU and its member states or from countries like the United States and Japan are involved in East and West Africa. Among other things, they may sponsor training courses, the secondment of experts or additional equipment for security agencies, yet knowledge about parallel efforts is often limited.[42] Moreover, coordination with local partners is also important to ensure that activities are actually useful in for day-to-day operations. Seminars or training courses, for example, have to be conducted when relevant personnel in recipient countries are available, not simply when instructors happen to visit the region.[43]

Finally, international organisations—notably the International Maritime Organization (IMO), Interpol or United Nations Office on Drugs and Crime (UNODC) which are all involved in efforts to improve maritime security in sub-Saharan Africa—need to coordinate their own efforts with other partners as well. It may also be advantageous when these organisations implement certain programmes because they are not merely regarded as an outside actor, trying to push a specific political agenda.

Non-governmental Organisations

As part of the security sector, maritime security is one of the core functions of any sovereign country. The role of non-governmental organisations is therefore limited to support in specific areas, yet they can play an important supplementary role. By and large, it is useful to distinguish between international NGOs which are active in East or West Africa—and, in some cases, both regions—and regional or domestic NGOs with a much more limited geographic focus.

Similar to other policy areas, international NGOs can try to lobby governments when they fail to act to address specific problems. Some of the most notable actions over the past decade have arguably been achieved in the fight against IUU fishing. Environmental organisations have conducted research on specific topics or even engaged in direct cooperation with government agencies. Some examples, such as the cooperation between Sea Shepherd and governments in Gabon, Sao Tomé and Principe or Tanzania, were outlined in Chapter 4.

Another interesting example is the Stable Seas project, funded by the One Earth Future Foundation. The US-based foundation began its involvement in maritime security in 2010 with the launch of the Oceans Beyond Piracy (OBP) project. OBP's main goal was to develop responses to pirate attacks against merchant ships by mobilising various stakeholders in the maritime industry and by helping to develop unique public–private partnerships. The annual 'State of Maritime Piracy' report, originally published to calculate the economic costs of Somali piracy, developed into a comprehensive analysis of human and economic costs of piracy and armed robbery at sea in different regions around the globe.[44]

At the same time, OBP's goals developed from a relatively narrow focus on the situation off the Somali coastline to a more comprehensive look at the constantly evolving issues of maritime security, underlining that any discussion about maritime security needs to include various topics and not simply focus on the problem of piracy. The logical next step was therefore an evolution into the more comprehensive Stable Seas project which 'engages the international security community with novel research on illicit maritime activities (…). These activities perpetuate organized political violence and reinforce each other to threaten economic development and the welfare of coastal populations'.[45]

There are other noteworthy examples of international NGOs which are involved in efforts to improve maritime security in general or specific aspects in particular. However, OBP's development from a project with a narrow focus on piracy towards a comprehensive programme that takes into account a diverse range of maritime security challenges exemplifies that the perception of these issues has changed dramatically over the course of the past decade.

Compared to international NGOs, domestic or regional organisations have a very different role. By and large, they are an essential part of the civil society, working as a link between specific groups and national governments. They are important as a forum for communication, but they are also needed for lobbying efforts, trying to promote the specific interests of their own members.[46] Some of the most prominent examples can be found in the fishing sector, largely due to the sheer number of fishing communities along the coasts of East and West Africa.

For many governments in both regions, domestic NGOs in the fishing sector are trustworthy partners for the sustainable management of fish stocks.[47] Furthermore, they can provide an intermediary function for law enforcement or naval personnel who are trying to tap into the knowledge of local fishermen. This role is often underestimated but should be considered as vital because it helps government agencies to address at least some of their resource constraints and provides them with additional information on all types of activities taking place in territorial waters and the EEZ.

Private Sector

Similar to NGOs, private companies and industry organisations are mostly able to play a role in specific areas related to maritime security. In the context of the topics discussed here, the sector should be divided into two different sets of actors. On the one hand, private security companies have become increasingly important for shipping companies and large oil companies involved in offshore production activities in recent years. Some security companies even cooperate closely with national governments or security agencies. On the other hand, companies involved in the exploitation of natural resources at sea as well as shipping companies are potential beneficiaries of improved maritime security.

The latter group is especially diverse. It consists of shipowners who operate a small fleet of vessels that are purely conducting coastal trade in East or West Africa, but also of international conglomerates operating different types of ships which are frequently calling at ports in both regions. Furthermore, oil companies and their suppliers own or operate many specialised vessels that are required for exploration or production activities offshore. Large trawlers, reefers and other ships involved in fishing activities are also generally owned by private companies which may be registered in East or West Africa or outside of either region.

These examples underline that the maritime environment is used for different types of economic activities, potentially leading to conflicting interests. All of the actors mentioned above—as well as other companies focusing on specific sectors such as deepsea mining or coastal tourism—stand to benefit from improved maritime security, yet their priorities are significantly different. Operators of merchant ships, for example, are not concerned by a lack of resources for agencies involved in the enforcement of fishing regulations. Subcontractors for the oil and gas industry are often only engaged in some countries and therefore not interested in regional initiatives. Owners of large fishing trawlers, on the other hand, may benefit from improvements in regional coordination. When fishing regulations are enforced stringently, they will be able to maximise their legal catches, giving them a competitive advantage over those operators without the necessary licences.

Overall, the term 'private sector' which is often used to describe organisations with a mainly commercial focus paints an extremely simplified picture of an incredibly diverse reality. At the same time, private companies—as well as their respective industry organisations—may try to promote their own requirements, yet these should be analysed in a broader context. Shipping companies, for example, have every right to be concerned about attacks against their ships, crews and cargoes. Compared to other maritime security issues, however, these may only be a limited concern for governments which have to balance limited resources and focus on their own priorities.

Private-sector organisations in general should also ensure that their own actions do not contradict their requirements. Most importantly, companies have to act decisively against corrupt behaviour by any of their employees. Their representatives are very unlikely to admit that bribes or facilitation payments are part of day-to-day operations in many countries throughout East and West Africa, yet most companies and industry organisations are quick to condemn such demands from staff at government agencies or other organisations.

Some shipping companies have become increasingly engaged in the fight against corruption in recent years. The Maritime Anti-Corruption Network (MACN) is the most visible example of these efforts. It was established in 2011 in a bid to eliminate corruption in maritime industries by 'raising awareness of the challenges faced; (...) collaborating with governments, non-governmental organizations, and civil society to identify and mitigate the root causes of corruption; and creating a culture of integrity within the maritime community'.[48] Even some large shipping companies that are MACN members, however, continue to keep internal records of acceptable payment levels in specific ports, ensuring that 'our masters to not pay over the odds when they go to countries like Kenya or Nigeria for the first time'.[49]

The private security industry is a specific subset of the private sector in general. For these companies, a lack of maritime security constitutes an opportunity to generate revenues. They are able to offer services in support of other organisations in the private sector and are often contracted by shipping or energy companies to protect their assets. Moreover, security providers can offer their services to national governments. Such public–private partnerships can be an effective method to address certain security challenges on short notice.

From a government point of view, it may be relatively expensive to contract private companies with security-related tasks. At the same time, such contracts can help to address shortcomings which might be even more costly in the longer term. Beneficiaries of enhanced security may even pay for such initiatives directly, albeit reluctantly. The cooperation between the Nigerian Navy and private companies operating patrol boats which are partly manned by naval personnel and then contracted and paid for by shipping or energy companies is a very good example.[50] In other cases, security companies could offer capabilities that national navies or law enforcement agencies do not possess at all, for example real-time tracking of different types of vessels or surveillance throughout the EEZ.

6.4 Summary

Attention for maritime security in East and West Africa has increased in recent years, yet there are no genuine maritime security communities developing in either region. Cooperation is improving, albeit from a very low level. In West Africa in particular, existing organisational structures are used to improve governance of the maritime environment and law enforcement in territorial waters and the EEZs of coastal countries throughout the region. Governments in East Africa have so far failed to employ existing organisations but the amendments to the Djibouti Code of Conduct, adopted in 2017, underline that political interest for maritime security issues is increasing in the region as well.

Sustainable improvements of maritime security will require efforts within a wider context, taking aspects like law enforcement and available resources for security agencies into consideration. Short-term results may be very limited but many challenges related to maritime security have rarely received any political attention in recent decades.[51] It would therefore be unreasonable to assume that problems such as piracy and armed robbery at sea, IUU fishing and extensive smuggling of various types of cargoes can be eradicated within just a few months or even years.

Improving maritime security requires a certain level of commitment from governments in East and West Africa. Most importantly, policymakers have to compile demands and capabilities from various stakeholders and include those in comprehensive maritime strategies. They should not be afraid or even embarrassed to address shortcomings which may be rectified later on, either on the domestic level or with assistance from neighbouring countries and international partners.

At the same time, maritime strategies on the national level are important to avoid technical or financial assistance that is based on the respective donor's priorities, not on actual needs in the recipient country. In the short term, it may be attractive to receive such assistance, highlighted by similar issues on land. Many governments in sub-Saharan Africa have even 'played a conscious role in securitizing their relationship with donors'.[52] Tangible results, however, are unlikely and it should be one of the main tasks for governments in East and West Africa to identify their actual requirements as long as they continue to rely on outside assistance.

Misguided priorities often have unwanted impacts. Security agencies in West Africa, for example, often receive assistance from their US or European counterparts to combat drug smuggling, yet the same agencies do not receive any assistance to address cigarette smuggling or illegal imports of pharmaceutical goods.[53] Concerns have been raised in the past, assuming that 'questionable data and selective narrative are being used to bolster support for a new campaign in the "war on drugs", which is likely to be as harmful and ineffective as previous ones have been'.[54] Perhaps more importantly, UNODC experts have highlighted that 'it would be difficult to imagine an issue of greater importance'[55] for people living in West Africa than the quality of imported pharmaceutical goods.

In East Africa, the international community's focus on counter-piracy operations might even have unwanted political consequences. In Somaliland, a region in north-western Somalia which strives to be an independent country, counter-piracy efforts have long been 'tied to the project of state recognition'.[56] Since 2013, the coastguard in Somaliland has received equipment and training from the European Union, despite the lack of a clear legal status for the agency. The relevant draft law only came into force in early 2019,[57] highlighting that the political will to build a functioning coastguard with the capability to conduct law enforcement tasks has been limited at best. Available resources may be extremely limited, but the immigration police in Somaliland—which has to deal with very similar challenges—has been described as significantly more effective, mainly due to prioritisation on the political level.[58]

These examples underline that maritime security challenges are often addressed without much regard for the broader context. For any government throughout East and West Africa, maritime security is merely one aspect of security in general. Addressing maritime security challenges in isolation may create shortcomings in other security agencies, while international assistance specifically for maritime agencies can lead to institutional rivalries. Government representatives have every reason to be desperate to avoid both issues, and it can easily be justified to opt for evolution rather than revolution in a bid to create sustainable improvements.

Finally, maritime security in sub-Saharan Africa should be recognised as different from other world regions. While government agencies may suffer from limited capacities, the private sector can help to address at least some of the current shortcomings. Public–private partnerships with companies in the security sector may be controversial, yet they offer a unique method to address a range of issues on relatively short notice. There is no question that such partnerships should be considered very thoroughly, but they should not be dismissed entirely by plainly insisting on the security monopoly of the state. Government representatives and partners from the private sector or from non-governmental organisations should rather find a way to improve coordination and to create frameworks that lead to improvements in maritime security, creating direct benefits for different stakeholders and—by extension—national economies and the general public.

Notes

1. See, for example, Alli, W. O. *The role of Nigeria in regional security policy.* Abuja: Friedrich-Ebert-Stiftung, 2012. 12–20. For a more comprehensive analysis of ECOWAS, see, Obi, Cyril. "ECOWAS_AU security relations." In: Hentz, James J. (ed.) *Routledge handbook of African security.* Abingdon: Routledge, 2014. 198–206. For a detailed look at ECCAS, see, Meyer, Angela. "Regional security cooperation in Central Africa." In: Hentz, James J. (ed.) *Routledge handbook of African security.* Abingdon: Routledge, 2014. 229–242.
2. Similar to the CRESMAC centre in Pointe-Noire where maritime security activities within ECCAS are coordinated, ECOWAS established the CRESMAO centre in Abidjan in 2018 (see, for example, Wassimagnon. 2018. Côte d'Ivoire: Abidjan, des experts en sécurité maritime de la CEDEAO en conclave pour parachever la dotation en personnels des CMMC et du CRESMAO. Koaci. Available at: https://koaci.com/cote-divoire-abidjan-experts-securite-maritime-cedeao-conclave-pour-parachever-dotation-personnels-cmmc-cresmao-122960.html). In March 2019, a memorandum of understanding for joint operations between Ghana, Côte d'Ivoire, Liberia and Sierra Leone was also drafted in March 2019. Improving cooperation between Ghana and Côte d'Ivoire was underlined by the detention of the product tanker ANUKET AMBER in December 2018 for alleged fuel smuggling between both countries (Personal interviews with naval officers from Ghana, Côte d'Ivoire and Togo, February–March 2019).
3. African Development Bank. 2011. *Eastern Africa: Regional Integration Strategy Paper 2011–2015.* ii. Available at: https://www.afdb.org/fileadmin/uploads/afdb/Documents/Policy-Documents/East%20Africa%20-%20Rev%20RISP%20.pdf.
4. Mathieson, Craig. *The political economy of regional integration in Africa.* Maastricht: European Centre for Development Policy Management, 2016. 7–11.
5. Personal interview with African Union representative, April 2016.
6. Blédé, Barthélemy and Walker, Timothy. 2016. Fulfilling the promise of the Lomé maritime summit. *ISS Today.* Available at: https://issafrica.org/iss-today/fulfilling-the-promise-of-the-lome-maritime-summit.
7. Blédé, Barthélemy. 2017. Fighting rising piracy in the Gulf of Guinea. *ISS Today.* Available at: https://issafrica.org/iss-today/fighting-rising-piracy-in-the-gulf-of-guinea
8. International Institute for Strategic Studies. *The Military Balance, "Chapter nine: Sub-Saharan Africa".* London: IISS, 2019. 438–502.

9. Ethiopia has a population of around 105 million, Kenya of around 50 million. For GDP data, see, World Bank. 2019. GDP (current US$). Available at: https://data.worldbank.org/indicator/NY.GDP.MKTP.CD?end=2017&start=2016.
10. Two prominent examples are the United Nations Office on Drugs and Crime's *Global Maritime Crime Programme*, expanded to West Africa in 2014, and the GoGIN project, co-funded by the European Commission and Denmark which started in 2016 and will run four years.
11. Murphy, Martin. *Contemporary piracy and maritime terrorism: The threat to international security*. Adelphi Paper 388. London: IISS, 2007. 16.
12. Tharoor, Ishan. 2009. How Somalia's fishermen became pirates. *Time*. Available at: http://content.time.com/time/world/article/0,8599,1892376,00.html.
13. Walker, Timothy. 2011. Stop dumping hazardous waste on Africa's shores. Institute for Security Studies. Available at: https://issafrica.org/iss-today/stop-dumping-hazardous-waste-on-africas-shores.
14. See, for example, Knaup, Horand. 2008. Prelude to piracy—The poor fishermen of Somalia. *Spiegel Online*. Available at: https://www.spiegel.de/international/world/prelude-to-piracy-the-poor-fishermen-of-somalia-a-594457.html; Glaser, Roberts, and Mazurek et al. *Securing Somali fisheries*. Denver: One Earth Future Foundation, 2015. 29–30; Nor, Mohamed Sheikh. 2019. Somali fishermen decry licensing Chinese vessels. Voice of America. Available at: https://www.voanews.com/a/somali-fishermen-decry-licensing-chinese-vessels/4734993.html.
15. Airahuobhor, Andrew. 2015. Is Nigeria's territorial water safe? *Daily Independent*. Available at: https://allafrica.com/stories/201502270895.html.
16. Anaeto, Emeka and Oritse, Godwin. 2018. Nigeria protests global piracy reports. *Vanguard*. Available at: https://www.vanguardngr.com/2018/08/nigeria-protests-imos-piracy-reports/.
17. Muyiwa, Lucas. 2019. Rising to the piracy challenge. *The Nation*. Available at: https://thenationonlineng.net/rising-to-the-piracy-challenge/.
18. Personal interview with representative from the Cameroonian maritime administration, April 2016.
19. Adam, Jean Paul. *The Blue Economy: Seychelles' vision for sustainable development in the Indian Ocean*. Speech at Chatham House, London, on 11 June 2014. Summary available at: https://www.chathamhouse.org/sites/default/files/field/field_document/20140611BlueEconomy.pdf.
20. United Nations Economic Commission for Africa. *Africa's Blue Economy: A policy handbook*. Addis Ababa: Economic Commission for Africa, 2016. 1.
21. More information about the topics discussed during the conference is available at: http://www.blueeconomyconference.go.ke.

22. Mooney, Turloch. 2016. Piracy and corruption stalk West Africa supply chains. *Journal of Commerce*. Available at: https://www.joc.com/port-news/international-ports/piracy-and-corruption-stalk-west-africa-supply-chains_20160407.html.
23. Maritime Anti-Corruption Network. 2018. Nigeria Collective Action—MACN Impact Report. 9. Available at: https://static1.squarespace.com/static/53a158d0e4b06c9050b65db1/t/5b603834f950b7af56780b0f/1533032513403/MACN+Nigerian+Report+Port+Toolkit+2018.pdf.
24. Jacobsen, Katja Lindskov and Nordby, Johannes Riber. *Maritime security in the Gulf of Guinea*. Copenhagen: Royal Danish Defence College Publishing House, 2015. 55.
25. Personal interviews with representatives of relevant government agencies in Cameroon, Ghana, Kenya and Senegal, April 2016–December 2017.
26. Personal interviews with representatives of companies in the shipping industry, November 2017–March 2019.
27. Alli, W. O. *The role of Nigeria in regional security policy*. 263–265.
28. This focus has been relatively comprehensively discussed in the academic literature, for example by: Francis, David J. *Uniting Africa: Building regional security systems*. London: Ashgate, 2006; Franke, Benedikt. 2008. "Africa's evolving security architecture and the concept of multilayered security communities." *Cooperation and Conflict*, Vol. 43:3. 313–340; Møller, Bjørn. *The African Union as a security actor: African solutions to African problems?* Working Paper No. 57. Copenhagen: Danish Institute for International Studies, 2009; and Gomes, Porto, J. and Engel, Ulf (eds.). *Africa's new peace and security architecture: Promoting norms, institutionalizing solutions*. London: Routledge, 2016.
29. Williams, Paul D. and Haacke, Jürgen. "Regional approaches to conflict management." In: Crocker, Chester, Hampson, Fen Osler, and Aall, Pamela (eds.) *Rewiring regional security*. Washington, DC: United States Institute of Peach, 2011. 49.
30. Buzan, Barry and Wæver, Ole. *Regions and powers: The structure of international security*. Cambridge: Cambridge University Press, 2003. 45.
31. Buzan and Wæver. *Regions and powers*. 53–54.
32. The concept was originally introduced by: Deutsch, Burrell, Kann, and Lee. *Political community and the North Atlantic area*. Princeton: Princeton University Press, 1957.
33. Bellamy, Alex. *Security communities and their neighbours: Regional fortresses or global integrators?* Basingstoke: Palgrave Macmillan, 2004. 17–27.
34. See, for example, Bøås, Morten. "Nigeria and West Africa: From a regional security complex to a regional security community?" In: Braathen, Einar, Bøås, Morten, and Sæther, Gjermund (eds.) *Ethnicity kills? The politics of war, peace and ethnicity in sub-Saharan Africa*.

Basingstoke: Palgrave Macmillan; Bah, Alhaji M. S. 2005. "West Africa—From a security complex to a security community." *African Security Review*, Vol. 14:2. 77–83.
35. Aning, Kwesi. "Identifying and responding to Africa's security challenges." In: Crocker, Chester, Hampson, Fen Osler, and Aall, Pamela (eds.) *Rewiring regional security*. Washington, DC: United State Institute of Peace, 2011. 150.
36. Personal interview with retired flag officer and former member of CTF 151 staff, May 2016.
37. Adler, Emanuel and Greve, Patricia. 2009. "When security community meets balance of power: Overlapping regional mechanisms of security governance." *Review of International Studies*, Vol. 35:S1. 69–72.
38. International Crisis Group. *The Gulf of Guinea: The new danger zone*. Africa Report No. 195. Brussels: International Crisis Group, 2012. 23.
39. The debates related to Ghana's integrated maritime strategy—ongoing at the time of writing—are a good example. Various government agencies were invited to provide contributions to the draft for the strategy, including among several others the Ghana Maritime Authority, the Ghana Navy, the marine police, customs and immigration services as well as the foreign ministry, the ministry for agriculture and fisheries and the national oil company, highlighting an extremely diverse range of stakeholders.
40. Raidt, John and Smith, Kristen E. *Advancing U.S., African, and global interests: Security and stability in the West African maritime domain*. Washington, DC: Atlantic Council, 2010. 49.
41. See, for example, Anderson, Mark. 2014. Aid to Africa: Donations from west mask '$60bn looting' of continent. *The Guardian*. Available at: https://www.theguardian.com/global-development/2014/jul/15/aid-africa-west-looting-continent; Shepard, Toby. 2015. How the United States makes corruption in Africa worse. Open Society Foundations. Available at: https://www.opensocietyfoundations.org/voices/how-united-states-makes-corruption-africa-worse.
42. Personal interview with maritime security analyst, January 2019.
43. Personal interview with Ghana Navy staff officer, May 2015.
44. An overview of the annual reports, first published in 2010, is available at: http://oceansbeyondpiracy.org/obp-reports?field_region_tid=All&field_obp_type_of_document_tid=254&field_obp_author_tid=All&field_subject_tid=All.
45. Stable Seas. 2019. Home. Available at: https://stableseas.org.
46. Mamattah, Titilope. "Building civil society in West Africa: Notes from the field." In: Obadara, Ebenezer (ed.) *The handbook of civil society in Africa*. Dordrecht: Springer, 2014. 143–156; Kew, Darren and Oshikoya,

Modupe. "Escape from tyranny: Civil society and democratic struggles in Africa." In: Obadara, Ebenezer (ed.) *The handbook of civil society in Africa*. 7–23.

47. Neiland, Arthur E. and Béné, Christophe (eds.). *Poverty and small-scale fisheries in West Africa*. Dordrecht: Springer, 2004.
48. Maritime Anti-Corruption Network. 2019. About MACN. Available at: http://www.maritime-acn.org/about-macn/.
49. Personal interview with representative from shipping company, October 2015.
50. This unique form of a public–private partnership has developed over time, largely based on demands from international oil companies looking to protect their offshore assets of Nigeria. The cooperation between the Nigerian Navy and private security companies is legally based on a Memorandum of Understanding (MoU), signed by a naval officer and a representative of the respective company. Contents of the MoU have been updated several times since 2012. At the time of writing, the most recent version of the MoU had been issued in March 2019 to 30 companies, all registered in Nigeria which is one of the key requirements stated within the document.
51. Potgieter, Johan and Walker, Timothy. "The 2050 African Integrated Maritime Strategy (AIMS): Content and progress." In: Mandrup, Thomas and Vrey, Francois (eds.) *Towards good order at sea: African experiences*. Stellenbosch: Sun Media, 2015. 97–99.
52. Fisher, Jonathan and Anderson, David. 2015. "Authoritarianism and the securitization of development in Africa." *International Affairs*, Vol. 91:1. 132.
53. For a brief look at the potential impacts of cigarette smuggling in West Africa, see, Doward, Jamie. 2013. How cigarette smuggling fuels Africa's Islamist violence. *The Observer*. Available at: https://www.theguardian.com/world/2013/jan/27/cigarette-smuggling-mokhtar-belmokhtar-terrorism. For a look at the impacts of smuggled pharmaceutical goods, see, United Nations Office on Drugs and Crime. *Transnational organized crime in West Africa*. Vienna: UNODC, 2013. 39–44. Overall, the number of related publications is limited, but the keynote speech during a high-level meeting on illicit trade in the ECOWAS region highlighted that such problems persist and have not been addressed in recent years (No author. 2018. Illicit trade: West Africa's USD 50 billion problem. Available at: https://www.stopillegal.com/blog/detail/illicit-trade-west-africa-s-uds-50-billion-problem).
54. Csete, Joanne and Sánchez, Constanza. *Telling the story of drugs in West Africa: The newest front in a losing war?* Swansea: Global Drug Policy Observatory, 2013. 13.

55. United Nations Office on Drugs and Crime. *Transnational organized crime in West Africa*. 39.
56. Dua, Jatin. 2011. Piracy and the narrative of recognition: The view from Somaliland. Social Science Research Council. Available at: https://www.ssrc.org/pages/Piracy-and-the-Narrative-of-Recognition-The-View-from-Somaliland/.
57. No author. 2019. Somaliland Coast Guard ready to exercise its powers across territorial waters. EUCAP Somalia. Available at: https://www.eucap-som.eu/somaliland-coast-guard-ready-to-exercise-its-powers-across-territorial-waters/.
58. Hills, Alice. 2016. "Off-road policing: Communications technology and government authority in Somaliland." *International Affairs*, Vol. 92:5. 1072–1076.

CHAPTER 7

Conclusion

Abstract This chapter summarizes the main findings presented in this book. It emphasizes that the blue economy includes many facets—ranging from coastal tourism to deep-sea mining—which have only been partly covered here, yet should be investigated for an analysis on the national level. That might be particularly useful because policymakers and academics alike have concentrated on few aspects of maritime security in recent years, especially piracy and armed robbery at sea. An increasing amount of research about IUU fishing is also available, but links between these two and other issues posing a challenge for good order at sea have not received much attention. Some recommendations for further research are also provided, including topics such as marine spatial planning or environmental aspects. These may not be directly relevant for maritime security, but they can help to solve long-term challenges and should therefore be an essential aspect during the development of any maritime strategy.

Keywords Maritime strategy · Marine spatial planning · Coastal tourism · Deep-sea mining

The previous chapters have provided an extensive look into the current state of maritime security in East and West Africa. Some aspects, notably IUU fishing, have only been touched upon superficially because a more in-depth analysis is beyond the scope of this book. Other facets, such as

D. Siebels, *Maritime Security in East and West Africa*,
https://doi.org/10.1007/978-3-030-22688-6_7

coastal tourism or renewable energy projects in the maritime environment, have not been included here at all. While these are currently not significant issues across either region, some individual topics are certainly relevant for specific countries or could develop into crucial aspects in the coming years. Forecasts for the spread of deep-sea mining along Africa's coastlines are one of the best examples.[1]

By and large, the research for this book has been conducted to compare and contrast challenges and issues related to maritime security that are relevant for both East and West Africa. Insights presented here are merely the first step, but they show some of the complexities that have to be overcome to improve maritime security in a sustainable manner. Moreover, the combination of publicly available data, academic research and a broad range of personal interviews and observations helps to address some of the gaps in the literature that is currently available.

As discussed throughout the previous chapters, academic research on any matters related to maritime security in sub-Saharan Africa was limited at best until fairly recently. Even today, specific topics such as piracy and armed robbery at sea, drug smuggling on maritime routes or—to a lesser degree—the extent and the potential implications of IUU fishing dominate the debate. Existing links between maritime security and economic development, possible areas for cooperation between security agencies and the private sector or the comprehensive input needed to draft a national maritime strategy are not receiving the same amount of attention.

The focus on a limited number of topics has led academics and policymakers alike to concentrate on a relatively narrow perspective of maritime security. In reality, the topic requires a broader look at links between various developments and actors in the maritime environment. These issues are increasingly important for economic growth and development, reflected in a growing recognition of the blue economy's potential which will hopefully lead to an accompanying academic debate in the coming years.

First and foremost, this book is aimed at widening the focus of debates related to maritime security in East and West Africa. It offers a valuable contribution to the academic literature, but it also has practical applications for various organisations which are somehow involved in deliberations about or the provision of maritime security.

Moreover, the book provides a positive definition of maritime security and a guide on how to apply that definition in practice. Related discussions are otherwise largely concerned with the implications of sea power or naval strategies, highlighted by the discussion in Chapter 2. Most navies around the globe, certainly those in sub-Saharan Africa, are largely involved in constabulary tasks, something that is rarely addressed in the existing literature. Potential dividends that investments in better maritime security can yield in the short, medium or long term are another topic that has not been discussed in much detail.

This book is not aimed at becoming a blueprint for any comprehensive maritime strategy on the national level. It does, however, offer a broad overview of aspects that should be considered in such a strategy and in an accompanying business plan which calculates the blue economy's potential and identifies key areas for investments.[2] Additional research will be necessary to inform related discussions in different countries. Some relevant observations, figures and considerations are already available, yet much more work is required to underline any arguments in discussions about maritime security in the regions covered in this book as well as in other regions around the world.

7.1 Recommendations for Further Research

Various areas can be identified to contribute to discussions about maritime issues in general and maritime security in particular. One important aspect for theoretical disputes is the future development of security communities in East and West Africa and the role of maritime security in this context. These have often been considered in the context of land-based security developments, but non-traditional threats such as drug smuggling and cyber crimes[3] or health crises like the recent Ebola epidemic in Guinea, Liberia and Sierra Leone[4] have also started to receive attention.

Maritime issues need to be included in this discussion, not least because of the close relationship between informal trade networks and smuggling problems[5]—both on land and at sea—which can be found in many parts of Africa. It is not exaggerated when the maritime environment is described as 'crucial for Africa's future'.[6] Moreover, it may be useful to apply a similar framework for debates about maritime security in other geographical regions such as Southeast Asia where many countries are facing challenges that are at least comparable to those in sub-Saharan Africa.

Another key aspect of this book is the relation between maritime security and the future development of the blue economy. Chapters 3 and 4 have addressed this area, showing that a lot of information needs to be taken into account. At the same time, data and further information related to many specific questions are still missing, and the quality of available statistics from most countries in sub-Saharan Africa is at least debatable.[7] Data is also often limited by the very nature of operations discussed in this book. They may involve commercial sensitivities—for example details about offshore oil production by certain companies—or even criminal actions, such as illegal fishing.

Researchers still have a lot of scope to further explore the links between economic development and maritime security on the national and the regional level. Better data and more accurate estimates would help policymakers to identify the potential value of enhanced maritime security for the outcomes of a maritime business plan. They would also help to further underline the conclusions in this book and provide arguments for investments into key areas. At the same time, the extremely diverse range of stakeholders who are relevant for such a maritime business plan or the subsequent maritime strategy has to be identified to include their views on these documents.[8]

Furthermore, the exact roles of different security agencies such as the navy, the marine police or the coastguard on the national level should be thoroughly analysed and compared with neighbouring countries. Identifying overlapping capabilities or gaps in the respective organisations' mandates is essential for regional cooperation. Different structures in the security sector are also an interesting topic for future research. Throughout East and West Africa, most countries have based the organization of their security agencies on models which were originally introduced by colonial powers, complicating multilateral or even bilateral cooperation. Studies on related issues in the maritime environment might offer further insights for land-based cooperation as well, for example to combat transnational organised crime or cross-border operations of insurgent and terrorist groups.

Environmental aspects have been largely disregarded for the purposes of this book. Long-term challenges caused by marine pollution or climate change may exacerbate existing or even cause additional security threats on land.[9] Such issues, however, are rarely considered to be a political priority. While that is a dilemma for many land-based environmental problems as well, the challenge in the maritime environment is even greater due to a lack of solid statistical baselines, such as the actual size of fish stocks. These issues may not be directly linked to maritime security, but security agencies—and navies in particular—often have an important role to play in providing the necessary platforms to conduct scientific research at sea in countries throughout East and West Africa. Moreover, these agencies should at least be aware of potential threats to include them in their strategic planning.

Finally, the possible involvement of private companies in the provision of maritime security has been mentioned briefly in this book, but deserves a lot more attention. Many academic articles have been written about the use of privately contracted security personnel on merchant vessels, a widespread deterrent used as a response to the increasing number of piracy attacks off the Somali coastline from 2008 onwards. However, there has been very little coverage of the potential for public–private partnerships to provide better security at sea. These are likely to lead to a broad range of ethical, legal and quite practical questions on different subjects.

Somewhat related, but slightly more philosophical, is a debate about the privatisation of security tasks in general. Due to the increasing availability of technical equipment, companies and non-governmental organisations are able to work in areas that have traditionally been regarded as the prerogative of security and law enforcement agencies. Commercial companies are already collecting information about the potential smuggling of oil products on behalf of clients from the private sector, while environmental NGOs are gathering surveillance data of fishing vessels without the explicit approval of responsible government agencies in the respective coastal countries. National sovereignty may therefore be claimed to avoid an official outsourcing of such tasks, but without the necessary capabilities, it is not much more than virtual sovereignty anyway.

7.2 Final Thoughts

As the previous section has shown, much work remains to be done to ensure that discussions about maritime security in East and West Africa are informed by reliable statistics and comprehensive information. At the same time, the necessary research would go a long way to address a widespread lack of transparency which often serves political purposes and creates the potential for corruption. While that is a problem in many other areas as well, specific research in the maritime environment is vital for two reasons. Available information is currently very limited, as shown throughout this book, while the blue economy offers a lot of potential for economic growth and development in two regions where population growth rates are often at a similar level or even higher than GDP growth.

Furthermore, it is crucial to address maritime security challenges in East and West Africa from a domestic point of view, not based on the agenda of outside actors. Discussions about corruption provide an important lesson in this respect. As explained in Chapter 6, corruption is an issue that is not limited to maritime security, but it has specific implications and characteristics in the maritime environment.

Addressing the related challenges requires efforts from a broad range of stakeholders, including foreign governments, international organisations and multinational companies. Corruption in Africa 'does not take place in a vacuum and is linked in complex ways to global actors',[10] highlighted by reports about the vast amounts of money that African countries have lost over the past decades due to illicit financial flows.[11] Any discussions about the scale of corruption in African countries from a purely Western perspective, on the other hand, would ignore the real nature of the problem and make it more complicated, if not impossible, to find sustainable solutions.[12]

Smuggling is another topic that looks very different from an international and a domestic perspective. Some related issues were briefly explained in Chapter 6, mainly underlining that outside actors generally focus on issues which may have an impact on their own interests. Efforts to combat cocaine smuggling in West Africa[13] or heroin smuggling in East Africa[14] serve to illustrate the point. These are largely aimed at disrupting trade routes that are used to transport illegal drugs to European countries.

Many other types of cargoes are also smuggled, yet the impact of these activities is by and large limited to the domestic level. In East Africa, sugar smuggling has been identified as a lucrative business for traders while governments are facing domestic job losses and losing out on customs revenues.[15] In West Africa, legal cargoes such as pharmaceutical products[16], fuel[17] or agricultural goods are often transported across borders without any knowledge of relevant authorities. In relation to rice smuggling into Nigeria, an officer from the Nigeria Customs Service even pointed out that 'smuggling is not just a crime, but the mother of many crimes'[18] because smugglers may use the same routes for items such as drugs or weapons.

Similar to corruption, smuggling is not solely a challenge in the maritime environment. The vast majority of imports to and exports from African countries, however, are transported on maritime routes, turning ports into vital hubs for trading and smuggling. Moreover, vessels suspected to be used in smuggling operations can often be identified based on certain operational patterns. Navies or law enforcement agencies would thus be able to concentrate their resources if they had the means to spot such patterns in the first place.

These are just two of many ways to illustrate that maritime security has to be addressed as an expansive set of very different challenges that are more or less linked with each other. Concentrating on just a few specific issues may seem to be less complicated, but efforts are very unlikely to be sustainable over time and might even create an unwanted displacement effect. When law enforcement agencies focus their efforts on the fight against drug smuggling, there are few—if any—resources left to combat other types of smuggling which might have much more immediate knock-on effects for the domestic population.

Overall, the involvement of actors from outside East or West Africa can certainly have positive impacts on maritime security. Similar to many other political areas, however, this involvement has so far been largely driven by the respective agendas of these outside actors, not by the attempt to find the often-cited African solutions to African problems. Ironically, many of those problems were caused by former colonial powers in the first place, going back to the infamous Berlin Conference in 1884 and 1885 during which virtually all of the borders that continue to pose problems until today were originally drawn on maps that still included a lot of unexplored areas at the time.[19] The outcomes from a European point of view were famously summarised by Lord Salisbury, one of the most influential British politicians at the time: 'We have been giving away mountains and rivers and lakes to each other, only hindered by the small impediment that we never knew exactly where the mountains and rivers and lakes were'.

African geography may be better known today. Problematic perceptions of Africa nevertheless persist. During the London Shipping Week in 2015, the author attended a seminar concerned with the threat of a re-emergence of Somali piracy. While most attendees agreed that the root causes for piracy are an 'African problem' that has to be addressed on land, the participants were almost exclusively middle-aged white men and not a single person in the room was from Africa, let alone from

Somalia. Such an event, hardly representative of the multinational shipping industry or a cosmopolitan city like London, is not very likely to find solutions that are a perfect fit for piracy or indeed any other 'African problem'.

Finally, it is worth highlighting once again that the blue economy offers vast potential. It can only be realised, however, if essential prerequisites such as a secure environment and good governance at sea are met. That requires the active involvement of all relevant stakeholders, particularly on the domestic level. Coastal communities, for example, may be negatively affected by offshore oil production or large infrastructure projects taking place in traditional fishing grounds. Some fishermen are then more susceptible to engagement in criminal activities, often simply in a bid to provide for their families. Governments therefore have to ensure that the involved companies provide alternative jobs or funds that can be used for relevant programmes.

Such connections have rarely been made in the past, but the situation is changing. Maritime security remains low on the list of political priorities, illustrated in different ways throughout this book. At the same time, the previous chapters have also shown that maritime issues are gaining more and more attention in many countries, helping to establish a climate that enables different actors to find and maintain solutions for many security challenges in the maritime environment. An African proverb therefore seems to be a fitting summary:

The best time to plant a tree is twenty years ago. The second-best time is now.

Notes

1. Misser, François. Deep-sea mining: Africa's new frontier. *Good Governance Africa*. Available at: https://gga.org/deep-sea-mining-africas-new-frontier/.
2. Siebels, Dirk. 2018. Protecting the 'blue economy'. *The Maritime Executive*. Available at: https://www.maritime-executive.com/magazine/protecting-the-blue-economy.
3. Aning, Kwesi. "Identifying and responding to Africa's security challenges." In: Crocker, Chester, Hampson, Fen Osler, and Aall, Pamela (eds.) *Rewiring regional security*. Washington, DC: United States Institute of Peach, 2011. 149–170.

4. Evans, Nicholas G. "Ebola: From public health crisis to national security threat." In: Lentzos, Filipa (ed.) *Biological threats in the 21st century.* London: Imperial College Press, 2016. 277–292.
5. Benjamin, Nancy, Golub, Stephen, and Mbaye, Ahmadou, Aly. 2015. "Informality, trade policies and smuggling in West Africa." *Journal of Borderland Studies*, Vol. 30:3. 381–394.
6. Gilpin, Raymond. 2016. Maritime safety and security: Crucial for Africa's future. *Africa Center for Strategic Studies—Spotlight.* Available at: https://africacenter.org/spotlight/maritime-safety-security-crucial-africas-strategic-future/.
7. For a comprehensive discussion about the lack of statistical capacity in countries throughout sub-Saharan Africa, see Jerven, Morten. *Poor numbers: How we are misled by African development statistics and what to do about it.* Ithaca: Cornell University Press, 2013.
8. Ghana was already named as an example in Chapter 6 because the discussion about an integrated maritime strategy was ongoing at the time of writing. Other examples include the Seychelles (Seychelles Ministry of Foreign Affairs. *The blue economy: Seychelles' vision for a Blue Horizon.* Victoria, 2014) or Benin (Blédé, Barthélemy. *Benin's maritime security challenges in the Gulf of Guinea.* Dakar: Institute for Security Studies, 2015. 7–9).
9. For an example about the potential effects of climate change on the movement of fish stocks across maritime boundaries, see Pinsky, Reygondeau, Caddell, et al. 2018. "Preparing ocean governance for species on the move." *Science*, Vol. 360. 1189–1191.
10. Hoffmann, Nimi, and Hendricks, Fred. 2018. "African perspectives on corruption." *Journal of Contemporary African Studies*, Vol. 36:4. 425.
11. Gossel, Sean. 2016. Africa needs to develop new ways of stemming illicit financial flows. *The Conversation.* Available at: https://theconversation.com/africa-needs-to-develop-new-ways-of-stemming-illicit-financial-flows-58892.
12. Apata, Gabriel O. 2018. "Corruption and the postocolonial state: How the west invented African corruption." *Journal of Contemporary African Studies* (published online).
13. Bish, Alexandre. 2019. The second coming of West Africa's cocaine trade? *Global Initiative.* Available at: https://globalinitiative.net/the-second-coming-of-west-africas-cocaine-trade/.
14. Haysom, Simone, Gastrow, Peter, and Shaw, Mark. 2018. *The heroin coast: A political economy along the eastern African seaboard.* ENACT Research Paper. Available at: https://enact-africa.s3.amazonaws.com/site/uploads/2018-07-02-research-paper-heroin-coast.pdf.
15. Rasmussen, Jacob. *Sweet secrets: Sugar smuggling and state formation in the Kenya-Somalia borderlands.* Copenhagen: Danish Institute for International Studies, 2017.

16. Asiedu, Kwasi Gyamfi. 2018. There's an opioid abuse problem unfolding in African cities and it's not getting the attention it needs. *Quartz Africa*. Available at: https://qz.com/africa/1223167/opioid-crisis-china-india-tramadol-flood-african-cities-in-ghana-nigeria-egypt-gabon/.
17. Kubi, Vincent. 2018. Ghana Navy arrests fuel smuggling syndicate. *Modern Ghana*. Available at: https://www.modernghana.com/news/856683/ghana-navy-arrests-fuel-smuggling-syndicate.html.
18. Ogunwusi, Bamidele, Utulu, Andres, and Nzeako, Ikechi. 2019. Smuggling: Drawback to Nigeria's rice revolution. *Independent*. Available at: https://www.independent.ng/smuggling-drawback-to-nigerias-rice-revolution/.
19. Michalopoulos, Stelios, and Papaioannou, Elias. 2012. The long-run effects of the Scramble for Africa. *Vox*. Available at: https://voxeu.org/article/long-run-effects-scramble-africa; Oduntan, Gbenga. 2015. Africa's border disputes are set to rise—But there are ways to stop them. *The Conversation*. Available at: https://theconversation.com/africas-border-disputes-are-set-to-rise-but-there-are-ways-to-stop-them-44264.

Index

A

Abidjan, 45, 49, 55, 122
African Continental Free Trade Area, 42
African Maritime Transport Charter, 35
African Standby Force, 12, 26, 86, 97
African Union (AU), 2, 12, 17, 18, 22, 24, 26, 27, 29, 35, 52, 74, 85, 86, 91, 97, 100, 103, 111, 122
Agenda 2063, 91
2050 AIM Strategy, 35, 91, 103, 104
Angola, 11, 26, 37, 38, 49, 78
Archipelagic nations, 92
Armed conflicts, 12
Armed robbery at sea, 3, 20, 75, 77, 81, 83, 102, 106, 107, 111, 113, 116, 120, 130
Artisanal fishing, 23, 58, 60, 61, 63, 70, 106

B

Bagamoyo, 47
Bakassi, 85
Benin, 33, 44, 45, 49, 50, 56, 75, 93, 137
Blue economy, 4–6, 25, 32–34, 48, 76, 84, 103, 104, 107, 108, 112, 115, 130, 131, 134, 136
Bottom-trawling, 61
Bull, Hedley, 15, 28
Burkina Faso, 10
Burundi, 11, 88
Buzan, Barry, 12, 13, 17, 18, 26–28, 109, 110, 124
Bycatch, 59, 61

C

Cameroon, 10, 11, 45, 46, 55, 82, 85, 87, 98, 124
Cape Verde, 10, 18
Central Africa, 11, 26, 82, 86, 122
Central African Republic, 11, 87
Chad, 10, 11, 18
China Overseas Fisheries Association, 60
Coastal communities, 3, 23, 58, 60, 61, 104, 106, 112–114, 136

D. Siebels, *Maritime Security in East and West Africa*, https://doi.org/10.1007/978-3-030-22688-6

Coastal states, 4, 10–12, 22, 61, 63, 64, 71, 84, 92, 106, 108
Coastal tourism, 2, 118, 130
Coastguard, 2, 4, 23, 33, 34, 58, 76, 77, 80, 95, 121, 132
Coastline, 2, 13, 44, 49, 50, 61, 67, 69, 74, 87, 91, 105–107, 116, 130, 133
Cold War, 14, 19, 27
Colonial powers, 16, 80, 85, 132, 135
Combined Exclusive Maritime Zone of Africa, 103
Comoros, 11, 12, 100
Contact Group, 99
Container terminal, 45
Corruption, 40, 43, 62, 93, 108, 109, 112, 115, 118, 119, 124, 125, 133–135, 137
Côte d'Ivoire, 34, 45, 55, 122
Cotonou, 33, 44, 45, 49, 50
Counter-piracy, 4, 22, 25, 40, 47, 55, 66, 84, 88, 89, 92, 111, 114, 121
CRIMARIO, 90, 100
Crude oil, 36, 38, 41, 49
Customs duties, 32, 37, 42

D

Dar es Salaam, 47, 56
Deep-sea mining, 130, 136
Djibouti, 11, 33, 51, 89, 90, 95, 96, 99, 100
Djibouti Code of Conduct (DCoC), 12, 13, 26, 47, 81–83, 86, 89, 90, 92, 102, 105, 114, 119
Djibouti Regional Training Centre (DRTC), 89, 90
Dredging, 45, 61
Drug smuggling, 120, 130, 131, 135

E

East African Community (EAC), 12, 15, 88, 98, 111
East Asia, 18
Economic Community of Central African States (ECCAS), 11, 12, 26, 82, 84, 86, 87, 98, 102, 104, 111, 122
Economic Community of West African States (ECOWAS), 10–12, 15, 26, 82, 84–86, 102, 104, 110, 122, 126
Egypt, 12, 13
Equatorial Guinea, 10, 33, 37, 59, 69, 85, 87, 98
Eritrea, 11, 47, 56, 88
Ethiopia, 11, 12, 18, 33, 47, 56, 85, 105, 123
Excess Defence Articles Program, 77
Exclusive Economic Zones (EEZ), 7, 20, 23, 25, 33, 34, 40, 49, 61, 63, 64, 67, 74, 108, 117, 119

F

Financial transparency, 2
Fisheries, 50, 60–63, 66–72, 86, 125
Fish-I Africa, 63, 65–68
Fishing
  grounds, 2, 22, 23, 58, 61, 68, 136
  industry, 24, 39
  patterns, 5, 58, 66, 113
  vessels, 2, 58–60, 62–66, 71, 86, 107, 108, 133
Fish stocks, 2, 3, 7, 23, 32, 58, 60–63, 66, 67, 75, 87, 107, 117, 132, 137
Flag state, 63, 64, 71
Food and Agriculture Organisation (FAO), 58, 64, 68

Food security, 58, 60–62, 67
Free-riding, 3
Functionalism, 15, 16

G
Gabon, 33, 37, 65, 85, 87, 116
GDP, 32, 36, 37, 45, 50, 52, 60, 67, 105, 123, 134
Gendarmerie navale, 76
Ghana, 6, 33, 34, 37, 44, 45, 51, 59, 60, 62, 67, 69, 70, 75, 93, 95, 122, 124, 125, 137, 138
Good order at sea, 20–22
Greenpeace, 72
Grotius, Hugo, 19, 29
Guinea, 59, 131
Guinea-Bissau, 59
Gulf of Guinea (GoG), 3, 55, 122
Gulf of Guinea Commission (GGC), 11, 26, 86

H
High seas, 19, 20, 64, 80, 83, 93
Hijacking, 38, 44, 53, 107, 114
Horn of Africa (HOA), 11, 12, 18, 51, 88, 96, 98
Hydrocarbons, 23, 36, 40, 58, 113

I
Illegal fishing, 5, 51, 58, 64, 68–72, 132
  operations, 58, 64, 132
  vessels, 2, 58, 64
Indian Ocean, 11, 12, 18, 22, 25, 46, 63, 66, 81, 88, 92, 99, 107, 114
Industrial fishing, 60, 66, 67
Inland waterways, 25
Institutionalism, 13, 15, 16
Intergovernmental Authority on Development (IGAD), 12, 85, 88, 99, 100, 111
International Maritime Bureau (IMB), 55, 78
International Maritime Organization (IMO), 43, 65, 71, 75, 81, 82, 89, 93, 95, 96, 99, 115
International oil companies, 37, 38, 126
International relations (IR), 13, 19
International Tribunal for the Law of the Sea (ITLOS), 63, 64, 71
Interpol, 6, 115
IORIS, 90, 100
IR frameworks, 14, 16
IR theories, 13, 14, 17, 18
ISPS Code, 19, 34
IUU fishing, 20, 23, 24, 33, 59–67, 72, 74, 75, 80, 81, 83, 86, 87, 93, 104, 106, 107, 109, 111, 114, 116, 120, 129, 130

J
Jordan, 12

K
Kampala Process, 87
Kenya, 11, 12, 33, 47, 51, 79, 88, 90, 95, 108, 119, 123, 124
Krasner, Stephen, 15, 28

L
Lagos, 44, 49
Lamu, 47, 56
Liberalism, 14
Liberia, 52, 86, 110, 122, 131
Lomé, 2, 33, 44
Lomé Charter, 103

M

Madagascar, 11, 12, 47, 56, 62, 63, 88, 90, 99, 100
Malawi, 11
Maldives, 12
Mali, 10, 18
Mare Liberum, 19
Maritime agencies, 61, 91, 105, 113, 121
Maritime Anti-Corruption Network (MACN), 118, 119, 124, 126
Maritime boundaries, 3, 20, 23, 34, 61, 87, 137
Maritime business plan, 33, 132
Maritime domain, 4, 7, 31, 34, 80, 82
Maritime Domain Awareness for Trade—Gulf of Guinea (MDAT-GoG), 78
Maritime governance, 24, 34
Maritime Organization for West and Central Africa (MOWCA), 86
Maritime remit, 4, 32, 50, 91, 106, 108
Maritime security
  challenges, 22, 33, 39, 45, 65, 111, 116, 120, 121, 134
  community, 109, 111
  complex, 109
  definition, 4, 10, 19, 21, 22, 24, 130
  issues, 4, 24, 31, 32, 40, 74, 75, 81, 82, 88, 91, 92, 102, 107, 116, 118, 120, 130
Maritime Security Centre—Horn of Africa (MSCHOA), 83
Maritime strategy, 22, 24, 33, 35, 62, 87, 104, 111, 113, 115, 125, 130–132, 137
Maritime trade, 3, 4, 19, 22, 23, 32, 33, 35, 41, 43, 45–47, 49, 54, 58, 107, 113
Mauritania, 3, 6, 10, 59
Mauritius, 11, 12, 18, 47
Mayotte, 11, 12
Mearsheimer, John, 14, 27
Merchant shipping, 2, 34, 66
Middle East, 12, 18, 56
Mozambique, 11, 33, 37, 39, 40, 51, 53, 54, 62, 63, 67, 70, 75, 87, 93, 104
Mukundan, Pottengal, 78

N

Nation state, 14–16, 85
Nato, 5
Natural gas, 38, 39, 41, 49, 52, 54
Naval personnel, 5, 76, 78, 106, 117, 119
Navies, 4, 5, 23, 33, 34, 50, 58, 61, 66, 75, 77, 80, 83, 90, 98, 106, 112, 119, 131, 133, 135
Neofunctionalism, 13, 16, 17
Niger, 10, 38, 39
Nigeria, 3, 6, 10, 14, 33, 38, 39, 46, 60, 66, 85, 94, 104, 106, 108, 119, 123, 124, 126, 134, 138
Nigerian Maritime Administration and Safety Agency (NIMASA), 107

O

Ocean governance, 22, 24, 137
Oceans Beyond Piracy (OBP), 94, 99, 116
Offshore assets, 23, 38, 50, 126
Offshore installations, 2, 33, 38, 48, 81
Offshore oil and gas
  deposits, 32, 40, 48
  exploration, 40
  production, 2, 4, 22, 23, 33, 36, 49, 104, 105
Oil rents, 36, 52

Oil revenues, 36, 37
Oman, 12, 47
Operation Albacore, 65, 71

P
Patrol boats, 2, 49, 106, 119
Piracy
  fight against, 12, 23, 89, 106, 114
  Nigeria, 75
  Somalia, 3, 20, 79, 80, 88, 105, 106, 114
  trials, 79, 81, 83
Pollution, 83, 132
Port operators, 32
Port State Measures Agreement, 65, 71
Power projection, 25
Privately contracted armed security personnel, 106
Private sector, 2, 5, 24, 40, 42, 50, 106, 112, 113, 118, 119, 121, 130, 133
Product tanker, 38, 44, 49, 122
Public good, 3, 34
Public–private partnerships, 106, 112, 116, 119, 121, 126, 133
Puntland, 87, 90

R
Realism, 13–15
Regime security, 14
Regime theory, 15
Regional Anti-Piracy Prosecutions and Intelligence Coordination Centre (RAPPICC), 89
Regional economic communities (RECs), 4, 10–12, 15, 18, 24, 35, 74, 82, 85, 86, 88, 90–92, 97, 102–105, 111, 113
Regional Fusion and Law Enforcement Centre for Safety and Security at Sea (REFLECS3), 89
Regional integration, 10, 13–16, 75, 82, 88, 102
Regional Maritime Information Fusion Centre (RMIFC), 88, 90
Regional security complex, 12, 13, 17, 18, 109, 110
Republic of Congo, 37, 46
Réunion, 11, 12
Revenues, 2, 23, 25, 32, 33, 36, 37, 39, 42, 43, 45, 48, 49, 58, 84, 92, 119, 134
Risk Intelligence, 44, 78, 94
Royalties, 32
Rwanda, 11, 88, 99

S
Sall, Macky, 62, 68
São Tomé and Príncipe, 3, 11, 18
Saudi Arabia, 12, 96
Seapower, 131
Sea Shepherd, 65, 71, 72, 116
Security cooperation, 14, 84, 86, 88, 98, 102, 104, 122
Security integration, 10, 13–15, 17, 25
Security vessels, 38
Senegal, 3, 6, 11, 38, 39, 46, 49, 53, 59, 62, 70, 75, 78, 93, 124
Seychelles, 11, 12, 18, 33, 75, 79, 89, 90, 93, 99, 100, 108, 111, 137
Shipping routes, 41, 49
Sierra Leone, 59, 122, 131
Smuggling, 2, 20, 75, 81, 87, 111, 120, 122, 131, 133–135
Somalia, 11, 53, 60, 69, 74, 75, 81, 85, 87, 88, 90, 92, 95, 105–107, 114, 121, 127, 136

Somaliland, 87, 90, 121, 127
South Africa, 12, 13, 40
South Asia, 18, 72
Southern African Development Community (SADC), 12, 26
South Sudan, 11, 12, 47, 88
Sovereign states, 13
Stable Seas, 92, 116, 125
SUA Convention, 20
Suakin, 47, 56
Subsidies, 66, 72
Sustainable Blue Economy Conference, 108

T
Tanzania, 11, 12, 33, 37, 39, 40, 47, 51, 56, 65, 71, 87, 88, 90, 104, 116
Tax base, 32, 42
Tema, 44, 55, 72
Territorial waters, 7, 20, 23, 34, 79, 80, 87, 106, 117, 119, 127
Till, Geoffrey, 19, 28
Toamasina, 47, 56
Toxic waste, 107
Tragedy of the commons, 66
Trawlers, 60, 61, 68, 69, 117, 118

U
Uganda, 11, 12, 18, 88
United Arab Emirates (UAE), 12, 56
United Kingdom Maritime Trade Operations (UKMTO), 83
United Nations Convention on the Law of the Sea (UNCLOS), 19, 21, 24, 34
United Nations Office on Drugs and Crime (UNODC), 72, 87, 94, 115, 120, 123, 126

W
Wæver, Ole, 12, 17, 18, 26, 28, 109, 110, 124
Waltz, Kenneth, 14, 27
Warships, 77, 80, 107
Western Africa, 10, 26
Westphalian era, 13

Y
Yaoundé, 11, 26, 46, 82, 96, 97
Yaoundé Code of Conduct (YCoC), 10, 11, 82–84, 86, 111
Yemen, 12, 90

Z
Zambia, 11
Zimbabwe, 11

The manufacturer's authorised representative in the EU is Springer Nature Customer Service Centre GmbH, Europaplatz 3, 69115 Heidelberg, Germany. If you have any concerns regarding our products, please contact ProductSafety@springernature.com

Printed and bound by CPI Group (UK) Ltd, Croydon, CR0 4YY
05/10/2026
02228153-0002